BEYOND MIERDA: THE CURSES, SLANG, AND STREET LINGO YOU NEED TO KNOW WHEN YOU SPEAK ESPAÑOL

TALK DIRTY
SPANISH

ALEXIS MUNIER & LAURA MARTÍNEZ

adamsmedia
Avon, Massachusetts

Published by
Adams Media, an F+W Publications Company
57 Littlefield Street, Avon, MA 02322. U.S.A.
www.adamsmedia.com

ISBN-13: 978-1-59869-768-1
ISBN-10: 1-59869-768-4

Printed in Canada.

J I H G F E D C B A

Library of Congress Cataloging-in-Publication Data
is available from the publisher.

This publication is designed to provide accurate and authoritative information with regard to the subject matter covered. It is sold with the unders-
tanding that the publisher is not engaged in rendering legal, accounting, or
other professional advice. If legal advice or other expert assistance is requi-
red, the services of a competent professional person should be sought.
 —From a *Declaration of Principles* jointly adopted by a Committee of the
American Bar Association and a Committee of Publishers and Associations

Many of the designations used by manufacturers and sellers to distinguish
their product are claimed as trademarks. Where those designations appear
in this book and Adams Media was aware of a trademark claim, the designations have been printed with initial capital letters.

Interior photos ©iStockphoto.com/Ray Roper, Luis Sandoval Mandujano,
Grafissimo, and Michael Cavén. Interior illustrations ©iStockphoto.com/
Matt Knannlein.

This book is available at quantity discounts for bulk purchases.
For information, please call 1-800-289-0963.

CONTENTS

SPANISH
READER
ADVISORY

To my one-of-a-kind grandmother Mane, who taught me the truth and wisdom that lie behind words.

—LAURA MARTÍNEZ

To my wise grandmother Marilyn, who couldn't care less about truth or wisdom but taught me the invaluable virtue of holding my tongue.

—ALEXIS MUNIER

Acknowledgments

A big thank-you to the Spanish and English speakers who got down and dirty for this book: Gio "Super Sexy" Moscioni, Paulo Muriti, Roelie Bottema, Toby and Karen Ernberg, Frédéric Heuer, and Andrès Pasquier. Thanks also to Jesus, the gorgeous son of Mexican migrant workers who rocked my sixth-grade world, and whose tight Levi's and limited English gave me my first dirty Spanish thoughts. On that note, I can't forget my husband Manu Tichelli, who helped tremendously with *Talk Dirty: Spanish,* even when I acted like a real *cabrona.*

—Alexis Munier

Special thanks to all of those who kept waking me up in the middle of the night to remind me of yet one more slang phrase I might have forgotten: the Mexico City troop Cuquita, Ady, Ricardo, Catus, Isabel, Richie, Romina and Gael; the New York Mexicans Carlos and Mariana; and Sandra Rubio, for reminding me that Spain is also a Spanish-speaking country. Gracias, Pierre, for the *bisous* and for staying close.

—Laura Martínez

Last but not least, thanks to our publisher, Adams Media, and their stellar team including wonder woman Paula Munier, her sidekick Brendan O'Neill, editor Katrina Schroeder, and copyeditor Heather Dubnick.

DISCLAIMER

All entries come with sample sentences as well

as common use and literal translations with the

exception of the dirtiest of the dirty.

You'll know them by

XXX: Too Dirty to Translate.

INTRODUCTION

Ah, *español*—the tongue of *toreros, tapas,* and *tequila.* Maybe you only had two years of high school Spanish, or maybe you don't know any but the words you learned while working the cash register at Taco Bell. No matter, if you don't already speak a fair amount of this feisty *lengua,* it's time to learn. *Español* is the third most widely spoken language in the world after Chinese and English, and it boasts the second highest number of native speakers— nearly half a billion. Whether getting around in Guatemala or cruising in Colombia, Spanish opens up a world of exciting adventures and opportunities.

But stick to your ordinary Spanish textbooks and you may miss out on a lot of what goes on around you. Spanish has evolved greatly throughout Latin America over the past several hundred *años.* So much so that the same expression used in Spain may get you arrested in Mexico! While an attempt to cover all the *jerga* in every Spanish-speaking nation would require many of books, *Talk Dirty: Spanish* has compiled *la crema y nata,* the cream of the crop.

You have two options when confronted with Spanish *jerga,* or slang: (1) Ask for repetition in your American-accented, schoolbook *español* and risk complete humiliation; or (2) respond clearly, making *amigos* and maybe even lovers. Without careful study of *Talk Dirty: Spanish,* the first scenario is inevitable. So turn on the *tango* music, hang your Picasso, fix yourself a couple of *tacos,* and get comfortable. *Talk Dirty: Spanish* is sure to be a heck of a ride.

CHAPTER ONE

Del caló al lunfardo:
A Brief History of Spanish slang

With Spain's exploration and colonization of the New World, *español* was brought to Central and South America and taken as far as the Philippines. There's even one former Spanish colony in Africa, Equatorial Guinea, which still lists Spanish as an official language. And can you name the U.S. state that has given Spanish official language status? Bet you couldn't guess—New Mexico!

Although Spain lost its Latin American colonies in the nineteenth century, the Spanish spoken throughout the continents continued to evolve. Many American Indians were killed or died of diseases brought by invaders, but native languages such as *náhuatl* in Mexico, *quechua* in Peru, and *guaraní* in Paraguay have made their mark on current speech as well. Today, all Spanish speakers may understand each other generally, but most countries and even regions have their own dialects and "dirty" Spanish. *Lunfardo*, a type of slang in Argentina, will be almost unrecognizable to a kid from Madrid. Likewise, a Panamanian might have a hard time deciphering the street talk in Mexico known as *caló*.

It's also worth noting that Spanish is not the only language spoken in Spain. *Basque, Catalan,* and *Galician,* among others, have contributed to Spanish as we know it. Influences on Latin American Spanish include the hundreds of thousands of African slaves who settled on the continent. In some places like Argentina and Uruguay, Italians and other Europeans who immigrated there during the nineteenth century also had a profound impact.

But the biggest influence of all has been, no surprise, the United States. American English has been widely adapted into Latin American speech, more so than in the *castellano* spoken in Spain. While in Spain there are Spanish equivalents to technical terms like "e-mail" (*correo electrónico*), in Latin America people mostly use the English word, *e-mail*. Besides technical terminology, American music and films are popular and have allowed English to make the deep imprint it has today on the Spanish language. A quasi-hybrid of the two languages now exists, known as "Spanglish." It's not just a disappointing Adam Sandler movie—Spanglish is a dialect spoken mainly by native Spanish speakers living in the United States, mixing words left and right. With one in ten U.S. households speaking Spanish at home, Spanglish is destined for success. In a hundred years, your family may be speaking it too!

Here is just a sample of English words in use in Spanish today:

el closet, el hall, el club, un speech, el living, el holding, los chips, el marketing, full-time, el stand, el e-mail, el mouse, el parking, el sandwich, los aerobics, el container, el drink, los pants, and *el sweater.*

CHAPTER TWO

¡Qué milanesas!
Introductions, Friends, and Family

When it comes to family members, Hispanics in general and Mexicans in particular have a complex relationship with their mothers. This can likely be traced to the influence of Catholicism in the *país*, where Mary and Mary Magdalene represent the two main visions of *mujeres*. With the choice of either virgin mother or whore, it's no surprise Hispanics have a complicated relationship with the women who bore them. *El padre*, on the other hand, enjoys a classic role as provider, ruling the roost. At least with large families, Mexican children have the opportunity to share both the blame and acclaim with their *hermanos* and *hermanas*.

agarrar la onda
to get someone, lit. to grab the wave
Yo creo que voy a cambiar de maestro de inglés; a éste no le agarro la onda.
I think I'll change English teachers; I just don't get this one.

4

¡Qué hongo!
What's up?, lit. What mushroom!
¡Qué hongo! Hace mucho que no sé nada de ti.
What's up? I haven't heard from you in a while.

¡Qué acelga!
What's happening? What's up?, lit. What chard!
¡Qué acelga! ¿Vamos al cine en la noche o qué?
What's up? Are we going to the movies or what?

¿Qué hubo? (also quihubo, quiubas, quiúbole, quihúbole, qué húbole)
What's new? What's up?, lit. What was there?
¿Quihubo? Hace mucho que no te veía por aquí.
What's up? I haven't seen you around in ages.

Other variations include:

¿Qué haciendo?
What's up?, lit. What's doing?

¿Qué hay?
What's cooking?, lit. What is there?

¡Qué milagro!
Long time, no see! lit. What a miracle!

¡Qué milanesas!
What's up?, lit. What pounded veal cutlets!

¿Qué onda?
What's up?, lit. What wave?

¿Qué pedo?
What is going on? What's up? What's happening?, lit. What fart?

¿Qué pez?
What's going on?, lit. What fish?

cuate, cuata (cuatacho, cuatacha) (Mexico)
friend, from Náhuatl (cuatl)
Con ese tipo ni te metas; es mi cuate.
Don't even mess with that guy; he's a friend.

chavo (Mexico)
guy, from Náhuatl
Ese chavo que trabaja en el banco me encanta, ¡pero no me pela!
I really like guy who works at the bank but he won't even look at me!
lit. I really like the guy who works at the bank but he doesn't peel me.

carnal, m
friend, lit. carnal
No hables mal de Pedro; es mi carnal.
Don't talk badly about Pedro; he's my friend.

hablando del Rey de Roma . . .
speak of the devil, lit. speak of the King of Rome
Hablando del Rey de Roma, ahí viene mi suegra . . .
Speak of the devil, here comes my mother-in-law . . .

hijo, hija
buddy/gal, lit. son/daughter
¡Qué onda, hijo! Vamos al hipódromo esta noche, ¿no?
What's up buddy! Let's go to the track tonight, okay?

mano, mana (manito, manita) (Mexico)
friend, buddy, lit. hand (little hand)
¡Vámonos de aquí mano, aquí nadie nos quiere!
Let's get outta here, buddy; nobody wants us around.

mina, f (Argentina)
girl, lit. mine (metal)
¡Qué mina más buena!
What a hot girl!

pana (Caribbean)
friend
Carrie tiene muchos conocidos, pero no son panas.
Carrie has lots of acquaintances, but they're not close friends.

pava, f (Spain)
girl, lit. female turkey
¡La pava ésa está buenísima!
That girl's gorgeous!

partir el turrón
to get to know someone better, lit. to cut the nougat candy
Vamos a tutearnos para partir el turrón
Let's use "tú" instead of "usted" to get to know each other better.

tío, tía (Spain)
mate, dude, lit. uncle, aunt
¿Qué hay tío?
Hey, dude, what's up?

viejo, vieja
pop, mom, lit. old man, old woman
Voy a pasar la navidad con los viejos.
I will spend Christmas with my folks.

La madre can be a lovely and affectionate person or a real pain it the neck. *Madrazo*, "big mother," refers to a big blow. *Caerle dea madre*, "to fall of the mother," is directed to an unbearable person. The mother is also a kind of reference or system of measurement: *un madral*, "a big mother," means a lot, while *una madrecita*, "a little mother," is something very small. In another field, *partirse la madre*, "to cut one's mother," means to work very hard. While *no tener madre*, "to have no mother," refers to individuals who are shameless, *¡qué poca madre!*, "what little mother," is given to people who have no consideration for others.

Mom is also connected with feelings and emotions. When happiness occurs or when something is cool, *a toda madre*, "to the whole mother" and *de puta madre*, "of the prostitute mother," are appropriate expressions. Emotions can also be negative and the expression quite rude, such as *¡Pa´ su madre!*, "for his/her mother" and also *¡puta madre!*, "prostitute mother"; both mean "f**k/damn!" "No f**king way" is translated into *¡Ni madres!*, "not even mothers."

Even when flirting in a pub, looking for *chicas,* you'll be facing *mamacitas*, "little mothers" or "hotties." If you feel your Oedipal complex is coming back, don't even think of drinking to forget who gave birth to you—it won't work. There will always be someone who'll say *estás mamado*, "you're breast fed," and another one who'll claim *estás hasta la madre*, "you're up to the mother," both meaning "you're drunk." Just give it up—*la madre* is here to stay.

CHAPTER THREE

De tripas corazón:
Body Talk

Hispanic women seem comfortable with their bodies, more so than their gringa sisters in the United States. No matter how *grande* or *pequeño* the bottom, you'll often see women in Latin America sporting tight jeans or revealing miniskirts. But in such seemingly conservative, Catholic nations, how is this possible? The answer is simple: like God, women's bodies are revered. Despite a good dose of *machismo* among Latinos, a woman's role as mother and wife is honored and respected. The female body is seen as the cradle of life, and no *contradicción* is found between flaunting that sacred vessel and honoring religious principles.

al pelo
just right, lit. to the hair
¡El pantalón que me regalaste me quedó al pelo!
That pair of pants you gave me fits just right!

a pedir de boca
fine, just right, lit. to ask by mouth
La junta con el cliente salió a pedir de boca.
The meeting with the client turned out just right.

9

ahuecar el ala

to get out of here, lit. to make a hole in the wing

Vayan ahuecando el ala; ya me quiero dormir.

Get out of here now; I want to go to sleep.

agarrar callo

to have experience, lit. to grab callus

Después de tres matrimonios, Miguel agarró callo con las mujeres.

After three marriages, Miguel has plenty of experience with women.

apechugar

to tolerate, lit. to breast

Si no traen el aire acondicionador esta tarde, vamos a tener que apechugar con este calor.

If they don't bring the air conditioner today, we'll have to tolerate this heat.

caerse la cara de vergüenza

to be very embarrassed, lit. to have one's face fall out of shame

Cuando se me salió el traje de baño, se me cayó la cara de vergüenza.

When my bathing suit slipped off, I was very embarrassed.

carne de gallina, f

goose bumps, lit. hen's flesh

Cada vez que Tito escucha esa canción se le pone la carne de gallina.

Every time Tito hears this song, he gets goose bumps.

coco, m

head, for one's mind to go blank, lit. coconut

Ya se me secó el coco de tanto pensar.

My mind went blank from thinking so much.

lit. My coconut went dry from thinking so much.

con la puerta en las narices

to send someone packing, lit. with the door on the noses

Rita le preguntó a su vecino si quería comprarle su coche viejo, pero éste le dio con la puerta en las narices.

Rita asked her neighbor if he wanted to buy her old car, but he sent her packing.

con el ojo cuadrado

to be very impressed, lit. with the square eye

Laura no sabía que su novio podía bailar así—se quedó con el ojo cuadrado.

Laura didn't know her boyfriend could dance so well—she was very impressed.

con el ojo pelón

to not be able to get any shuteye, lit. with the bold eye

Mateo estaba tan preocupado por su amigo que pasó toda la noche con el ojo pelón.

Mateo was so worried about his best friend that he wasn't able to get any shuteye all night.

como anillo al dedo

to fit perfectly, lit. like a ring to the finger

Este trabajo que Sandra consiguió, le cayó como anillo al dedo.

This job Sandra just got fits her perfectly!

comerse a alguien con los ojos
to ogle, lit. to eat somebody with the eyes
El muchacho lleva horas comiéndose a la bailarina con los ojos.
The guy has been ogling that dancer for hours!

con una mano por delante y otra por detrás
to be dirt poor, lit. with one hand in front and the other in back
La familia mexicana de la cuadra llegó a este país con una mano por delante y otra por detrás.
The Mexican family in the neighborhood arrived in this country dirt poor.

con uñas y dientes
to defend something fiercely, lit. with nails and teeth
Carmen defendió a su novio con uñas y dientes.
Carmen stood by her boyfriend and defended him fiercely.

cortarse un huevo y la mitad del otro
to bet one's life, lit. to cut one ball and half the other (Mexico)
Me corto un huevo y la mitad del otro que ese tío español me invita a bailar.
I bet my life that cute Spanish guy is going to ask me to dance!

dar cuello
to fire somebody, lit. to give neck
A la maestra le dieron cuello por andar con el director.
The teacher got fired because she was dating the principal.

dar el brazo a torcer

to cave in, lit. to give one's arm to be twisted

No quería reconocer que fue su culpa, pero al final, dio su brazo a torcer.

He didn't want to admit that it was his fault, but in the end he caved in.

de dientes para afuera

insincere, lit. from the teeth outwards

Todas esas cosas lindas que me dijo mi primer novio fueron de dientes para afuera.

All those pretty things my first boyfriend told me were insincere.

echar de cabeza

to incriminate / betray somebody, lit. to throw off the head

En medio de la discusión, Donna echó a su hijo de cabeza y le dijo a la policía que él se había robado el dinero.

In the middle of the discussion, Donna betrayed her son and told the police that he was the one who stole the money.

echar en cara

to throw something back in someone's face

Le conté toda mi vida y luego me lo echó en cara.

I told her my life story and then she threw it back in my face.

echar una cana al aire

to have an affair / to have a bit of fun, lit. to throw a white hair in the air

María aprovechó el fin de semana en París para echarse una cana al aire con un francés.

Maria took advantage of a weekend in Paris to have an affair with a Frenchman.

13

echar una pestaña

to take a nap, lit. to throw an eyelash away

Estoy tan cansado, que esta tarde me voy a echar una pestaña.

I am so tired that I'll take a nap this afternoon.

hablar hasta por los codos

to talk nonstop, lit. to speak even from the elbows

Mi abuela habla hasta por los codos.

My grandmother talks a lot!

hacerse de la boca chiquita

to play the supermodel, lit. to make oneself of the small mouth

No te hagas de la boca chiquita; sé que te fascina comer pastel.

Don't play the supermodel; I know you love to eat cake.

hacer la barba

to suck up to someone, lit. to make the chin

Jorge de contabilidad siempre le está haciendo la barba al jefe.

Jorge in accounting is always sucking up to the boss.

hacerla de pedo

to make a big fuss, lit. to make a fart of it

¡Voy a terminar con mi novia, porque siempre la está haciendo de pedo!

I am going to break up with my girlfriend because she is always making a big fuss!

hacerse de la vista gorda

to turn a blind eye, lit. to pretend to have fat sight

Verónica vio a su marido con otra mujer, pero se hizo de la vista gorda.

Veronica saw her husband with another woman, but she turned a blind eye.

hacer de su culo un papalote

to do whatever the hell one wants, lit. to make a kite out of one´s ass

No me importa si van a la playa o a las montañas; hagan de su culo un papalote.

I don't care if you go to the mountains or to the beach; you can do whatever the hell you want.

hacer de tripas corazón

to let bygones be bygones, lit. to make a heart out of the intestines

Aunque ella me trató mal la primera vez que salimos, hice de tripas corazón y la llamé otra vez.

Even though she treated me badly the first time we went out, I let bygones bye bygones and called her up again.

lavar el coco

to brainwash, lit. to wash the coconut

Los del nuevo culto ya le lavaron el coco a todo el vecindario.

A new cult has brainwashed the entire neighborhood.

llantas, mpl

love handles, lit. tires

Ya no comas tanto José; mira cómo tienes las llantas.

You shouldn't eat so much José; look at your love handles.

maceta, f

head, lit. flower pot

No le hagan caso a mi mamá; está mal de la maceta.

Don't listen to my mom; she's sick in the head.

malas lenguas, fpl

gossipers, lit. bad tongues

¡No hagas caso lo que digan las malas lenguas!

Don't listen to gossipers!

mala pata, f

bummer, bad luck, lit. bad leg

¡Qué mala pata! No nos tocó juntos en el avión.

What a bummer! We didn't get seats together on the plane.

doblar las manos

to give in, lit. to bend the hands

¡Nunca dobles las manos! ¡Combate a tu enemigo hasta la muerte!

Never give in! Fight your enemy to the death!

pasársele a alguien la mano

to go over the top, lit. to pass one's own hand

Carlos hizo bien regañando al perro, pero se le pasó la mano al quitarle la comida y el agua.

Reprimanding his dog was okay, but Carlos went over the top when he took away his food and water.

meter en cintura

to get someone in line, lit. to put inside the waist

Los niños se rebelaron contra la niñera, pero ella los metió en cintura.

The babysitter got the kids in line.

meter la pata

to screw up, lit. to put the foot in

Ya metí la pata; le dije al maestro que no estuve enfermo ayer.

I screwed up and told my teacher I wasn't sick yesterday.

morderse un huevo

to handle a difficult situation, lit. to bite one's ball (egg)

Me tuve que morder un huevo, pero le dije que no quería volver a verla.

It was a very difficult situation to handle, but I told her I didn't want to see her again.

no pegar un ojo

to not be able to sleep, lit. to not be able to stick an eye

Había tanto ruido afuera que no pude pegar un ojo.

It was so noisy outside that I wasn't able to sleep.

no tener tres dedos de frente

to not be very smart, lit. to not have three fingers of forehead

Esa niña será muy bonita, pero no tiene tres dedos de frente.

That girl might be pretty but she's really not very smart.

parar oreja

to listen / pay attention, lit. to stop the ear

Para oreja; ya van a anunciar los ganadores.

Pay attention; they're about to announce the winners.

planchar oreja

to sleep, lit. to iron ear

El viaje fue tan largo que paramos en el camino a planchar oreja.

The trip was so long that we stopped along the way to sleep.

pelar el diente

to smile, lit. to peel the tooth

Mi hermana siempre sale en las fotos pelando el diente.

My sister always smiles in photos.

piel chinita

goose bumps, lit. little Chinese flesh

**Cuando mi novio me declaró su amor, se me puso la
    piel chinita.**

*When my new boyfriend declared his love to me, I got goose
    bumps.*

pluma, f

fart, lit. feather/pen

¡Qué feo huele! Alguien se echó una pluma.

It stinks! Someone farted.

no tener un pelo de tonto

to be no fool, lit. to not have one hair of silly person

Sandro no tiene un pelo de tonto.

Sandro is no fool.

no tener pelos en la lengua

to speak one's mind, lit. without hairs in the tongue

**Mi abuelo siempre dice lo que siente; no tiene pelos en
    la lengua.**

My grandfather always says what he thinks; he speaks his mind.

sudar la gota gorda

to make an extra effort / work hard, lit. to sweat a fat drop

Pasé el examen de matemáticas, pero sudé la gota gorda.

I passed the math test, but I really suffered for it.

taparle el ojo al macho

to do something without meaning it, lit. to cover the eye of the macho

Juan fue a la iglesia pero sólo para taparle el ojo al macho.

Juan only went to church only to show off.

tener la cola sucia

to know one did something wrong, lit. to have the ass dirty

Es por eso que mi prometido me regaló un ramo de rosas; ¡sabe que tiene la cola sucia!

That's why my fiancé gave me a bouquet of roses! He knows he did something wrong.

tener cola que te pisen

to have something to be ashamed of, lit. to have a tail to be stepped on

Rick no se atreve a criticarnos, porque él también tiene cola que le pisen.

Rick doesn't dare criticize us because he also has something to be ashamed of.

tomar el pelo

to pull someone's leg, lit. to take someone's hair

No creas nada de lo que te dice el payaso; te está tomando el pelo.

Don't believe anything the clown tells you; he's pulling your leg.

uña y carne

to be two peas in a pod, lit. fingernail and flesh

Yo me llevo muy bien con mi suegra; somos uña y carne.

I get along very well with my mother-in-law; we are two peas in a pod!

CHAPTER FOUR

Por si las moscas: Awakening the Animal Within

Whether or not you believe in evolution, a lot of people act like *animaes*. Hence the multitude of idioms, expressions, and *jerga* involving the animal world in Spanish. From monkeys to mice and birds to bugs, you'll find a perfect fit to describe the behavior of most people you know. Some expressions have negative connotations and are meant to shame the guilty parties into improving their behavior, while others merely seem to state a comparison. It's up to you to decide which phrase is most appropriate to get your annoying co-worker to shut up or your *coñazo* brother to give back the CDs of yours he never returned.

andar a otro perro con ese hueso

to tell somebody who cares, lit. to go to another dog with that bone

Esa historia no te la creo; vete a otro perro con ese hueso
I don't believe that story; go and tell it to somebody who cares.

agarrar de puerquito

to have it in for someone, lit. to grab someone like a little pig

La maestra ya agarró a Paulo de puerquito.

The teacher has it in for Paulo.

buscarle tres pies al gato

to complicate things, lit. to look for three feet on a cat

Así son las cosas; no le busques tres pies al gato.

It is what it is; don't complicate things!

cabro, cabra (Chile)

young kid, lit. young goat

El parque estaba lleno de cabros chicos.

The park was full of young kids.

cada chango a su mecate

to each his or her own thing, lit. each monkey to its leash

A mi no me metan en sus asuntos; cada chango a su mecate.

Don't mix me up in your things; each one to his or her own thing.

como burro sin mecate

uncontrollable, lit. like a donkey without leash

Desde que la esposa de Ricardo se fue, anda como burro sin mecate.

Ever since Ricardo's wife left him, he's been uncontrollable.

como Dios puso al perico

to tell someone off, lit. like God did to the parrot

La mamá de Rodrigo lo puso como Dios al perico por llegar tan tarde a la escuela.

Rodrigo's mother told him off for being so late to school.

como el cangrejo

to go backwards, lit. like the crab

**Esta familia nunca progresa; va como el cangrejo,
para atrás.**

This family never progresses—it moves backwards.

como pez en agua

in one's element, comfortable, lit. like fish in water

**A sólo tres días de empezar el nuevo trabajo, Claudia
ya se sentía como pez en agua.**

*Only three days after she started her new job, Claudia was on
her own.*

quedarse como el perro de las dos tortas

to be left with neither one nor the other, lit. to be left like the
dog of the two sandwiches

**Las dos chicas abandonaron a León y él se quedó como
el perro de las dos tortas.**

*Both girls abandoned Leon and he was left with neither one
nor the other.*

como la caca del perico

a worthless piece of shit, lit. like the parrot's shit

**Este tipo no es bueno para ti, Sarah; es no más como la
caca del perico.**

That guy is no good for you, Sarah. He's a worthless piece of shit.

poner a alguien como lazo de cochino

to tell someone off, lit. to put someone like a pig's rope

La esposa de Raul lo puso como lazo de cochino.

Raul's wife really told him off.

coyotito, m

siesta/nap, lit. small coyote

Estaba tan cansada que me eché un coyotito en la oficina.

I was so tired, I took a little nap at work.

con la cola entre las patas

with one's tail between one's legs

Hernán regresó con la cola entre las patas a pedirle perdón a Maya.

Hernán came back with his tail between his legs to ask for Maya's forgiveness.

dar gato por liebre

to rip someone off, lit. to give a cat instead of a hare

El dueño de la bodega me dio gato por liebre.

The bodega owner ripped me off.

darle palos a su perro

to hurt nobody but oneself, lit. to hit one's dog

Cuando José testificó en su contra, le dio palos a su perro.

When Jose testified in his own defense, he incriminated nobody but himself.

hacer de aguilita

to pee squatting, lit. to make like a little eagle

El baño estaba tan sucio que tuvimos que hacer de aguilita.

The toilet was so dirty that we had to pee squatting.

IMMIGRATION OFFICER
(3298)
24 MAY 2003

23

dar el gatazo

to look okay, lit. to give the big cat

Los zapatos no son nuevos, pero como la boda es de noche, seguro dan el gatazo.

The shoes aren't new but since the wedding is at night, they'll look okay.

el burro hablando de orejas

the pot calling the kettle black, lit. the donkey speaking about ears

Alexis dice que sus hermanos son muy flojos; ¡es el burro hablando de orejas!

Alexis says her brothers are lazy bums. That's the pot calling the kettle black!

en menos que canta un gallo

in the shake of a lamb's tail, lit. quicker than a rooster singing

Este coche te lo arreglo en menos que canta un gallo.

I can fix your car in the shake of a lamb's tail.

feliz como una lombriz

happy as a clam, lit. happy as a worm

Desde que tiene novio, mi hermana está feliz como una lombriz.

Ever since she got herself a boyfriend, my sister is as happy as a clam.

echarse un gallo (Mexico)

to spit a loogie, lit. to spit a rooster

¡Ni se te ocurra echarte un gallo en la alfombra!

Spit a loogie on the carpet and you'll be sorry!

llevar gallo a alguien (Mexico)
to serenade, lit. to take a rooster to someone
Antes de declararse a su novia, Juanito contrató un violinista para llevarle gallo a su novia.
Just before Juanito proposed, he arranged for a violinist to serenade his girlfriend.

gata, f (Mexico)
maid, lit. female cat
Daniel dice que su gata está bien buena.
Daniel says his maid is really hot.

gato encerrado, m
something fishy, lit. locked-up cat
En todo este asunto hay gato encerrado.
There is something fishy going on here.
lit. In this whole business there is a locked-up cat.

hacerse pato
to feign ignorance, lit. to make oneself a duck
No te hagas pato; el tendero vio cuando te robaste la fruta.
Don't feign ignorance; the shopkeeper saw you steal the fruit.

hacer el oso
to make an ass of oneself, lit. to make the bear
Anoche me puse muy borracho y terminé haciendo el oso
Last night I got so drunk I made an ass of myself.

la misma gata pero revolcada

basically the same, lit. the same cat but knocked down

Vi la segunda parte de la película. Es la misma gata pero revolcada.

I saw the sequel to the movie. It's basically the same as the first one.

marca patito, f

schlock, lit. trademarked little duck

El colchón que me compré de segunda mano es marca patito.

The mattress I bought secondhand is schlock.

hacer manita de puerco

to force something out of someone, lit. to make a little hand of pork

Le tuvimos que hacer manita de puerco pero al final confesó.

We had to force it out of him, but he finally confessed.

mosquita muerta, f

ice queen, lit. little dead fly

¡Cuidado con Salma! Parece que es simpática, pero es una mosquita muerta.

Beware of Salma! She looks nice, but she's an ice queen.

no pasar de perico perro

to not work enough to improve one's situation, lit. to not pass parrot dog

Mi primo no quiere estudiar; así nunca va a pasar de perico perro.

My cousin doesn't want to go to school—he'll never work hard enough to improve his situation.

orejas de cochino, plf

to pretend you don't hear, lit. pig's ears

Le dije que se cambiara de lugar pero se hizo orejas de cochino.

I told him to change seats but he pretended not to hear me.

paloma blanca, f

innocent as a dove, lit. white dove

El chico es un ladrón, pero su mamá cree que es una blanca paloma.

The kid is a thief, but his mom thinks he's innocent as a dove.

papando moscas

day dreaming, lit. catching flies

Siempre están papando moscas.

You're always day dreaming.

pelar gallo

to die, lit. to pluck rooster

El viejo firmó el testamento antes de pelar gallo.

The old man signed his will before dying.

ponerse color de hormiga

to get worse, lit. to turn the color of an ant

Cuando llegó la policía, la situación se puso color de hormiga.

When the cops arrived, the situation only got worse.

ponerse trucha (Mexico)

to pay attention, lit. to act like trout

Pónte trucha porque sólo te voy a explicar esto una sola vez.

Pay attention because I am going to explain this only once.

ponerse águila

to pay attention!, lit. to act like an eagle

¡Pónte águila! Ya van a anunciar el número ganador.

Pay attention! They 're about to announce the winning numbers.

ponerse chango

to be alert, lit. to act like a monkey

**Hay que ponerse chango y escuchar los números
del Bingo.**

You've got to be alert to hear the numbers at the Bingo.

andar de pata de perro

to be out and about, lit. to walk on dog's leg

**A mi mamá nunca la encuentras en casa; siempre anda
de pata de perro.**

My mom is never at home; she is always out and about.

por un pelo de gato

by just a hair, lit. by the hair of a cat

Nos salvamos del huracán por un pelo de gato.

We were spared from the hurricane by just a hair.

por si las moscas

just in case, lit. for if the flies

Voy a guardar este documento, por si las moscas.

I will save this document, just in case.

un ojo al gato y otro al garabato

to always have an eye on our property, lit. one eye to the cat,
the other one to the scribble

**Clara nunca descuidó su paraguas durante la obra;
estaba con un ojo al gato y otro al garabato.**

Clara never took her eye off her umbrella during the play.

CHAPTER FIVE

Hijos de la tostada:
Nouns and Adjectives to Flatter and to Insult

In the summer of 2007, Spain appeared unable to take a joke. After a cartoon was published mocking the heir to the Spanish throne, Felipe, magazines containing the offensive material were seized by police around Madrid. Was Spain just having a bad day, or was this truly an insult to the royal *familia*? The country had just passed a law to increase the birthrate by giving families around 2,500 euros per child. The cartoon depicted Felipe making love to his wife, Letizia, shouting, "Do you know what this means if you get pregnant? It will be the closest thing to work I've ever done!"

In an odd twist, a prime example of flattery that seems strange to most Americans is the tradition of *El Caganer* ("the shitter," in Catalan) in the Spanish province of Catalonia. That's right, little statues of famous people and characters hunched over taking a poop can be found all over the region at Christmastime. The same year the Prince and his wife were married, a figure of them in *Caganer* style appeared. Rather than being removed, the royal family was flattered. *El Caganer* is an ancient sign of fertility and thus a portent of good luck. Considering the couple has had two *niñas* in just three years, the statue seems to be working.

Let this serve as a reminder: insults are fine, as long as they appear to be flattery . . .

abusado, abusada
very smart, lit. abused

Ese muchacho es muy abusado; se saca diez en todas las materias.

That kid is really smart; he always gets straight As at school.

acelerado, acelerada
hyper, frantic, lit. accelerated

Me cae muy bien esa chava, pero es un poco acelerada.

I like that girl a lot but she's a little hyper.

agachado, agachada
humble, lit. bent over

Los trabajadores de la fábrica nunca protestan por sus derechos; son unos agachados.

The factory workers never complain about their situation; they are very humble.

apretado, apretada
arrogant/presumptuous/snobbish, lit. tight

Las chavas de mi colonia son todas unas apretadas.

The girls from my neighborhood are all snobbish.

arrastrado, arrastrada
subservient, lit. dragged on/swept out

Jaimito es el consentido del jefe, porque es bien arrastrado.

Jaimito is the boss's favorite because he is very subservient.

aventado, aventada

audacious/bold, lit. thrower

A ese chavo no le da miedo nada; es un aventado.

That guy is not scared of anything; he is very audacious.

baboso, babosa (Mexico)

airhead, lit. drooler

¡Esa rubia bonita es una babosa!

That pretty blonde is such an airhead!

barbero (Mexico)

ass-kisser/suck-up, lit. barber

¡No seas tan barbero!

Don't be such an ass-kisser!

boludo, m (Argentina)

stupid, lit. big-balled

¿Cómo pudiste perder tu billetera? ¡Eres un boludo!

How could you lose your wallet? You're so stupid!

bolsón, m

lazy bum, lit. big bag

Ya van tres días que no vas a la escuela, ¡eres un bolsón!

You haven't been to school in three days; you are such a lazy bum!

burro, m

stupid, dumb, lit. donkey

Esos niños no aprenden nada en la escuela; ¡son unos burros!

Those kids don't learn anything at school; they're really dumb!

31

büey, m
stupid, lit. bull
Mi maestro de matemáticas es bien büey.
My math teacher is really dumb.

cabeza hueca, f
knucklehead, lit. hollow head
**¡Qué cabeza hueca! Andrés olvidó apagar la plancha
esta mañana y quemó la casa.**
*What a knucklehead! Andrés forgot to turn the iron off this
morning and burned the house down!*

caradura, f
someone who has a lot of nerve, lit. hard-face
A todo mundo le está pidiendo dinero ese caradura!
She's asking everybody for money, what nerve!

comemierda, f
shithead, lit. shit-eater
El jefe de contabilidad es un comemierda.
The chief of accounting is a total shithead.

corriente
ordinary, common, lit. current
**No te juntes con los nuevos chicos de la cuadra; son
unos corrientes.**
Don't mix with the new kids on the block; they're too common.

cara de palo, f
to look very serious, lit. face of a stick
¿Qué te pasa? ¿Por qué esa cara de palo?
What's wrong? Why do you look so serious?

cabrón, m

son of a bitch, lit. goat (from slang meaning of goat: cuckold)

¡Se fue con otra ese cabrón!

He ran away with another woman, that son of a bitch!

cabrona, f

bitch, lit. goat (female cuckhold)

¡Se fue con otro la cabrona!

She ran away with another man, the bitch!

conchudo, conchuda

shameless/lazy, lit. with a shell

No seas conchudo; ayúdale a tu hermana a recoger los platos.

Don't be so lazy. Help your sister clear the table.

cuatro ojos

four-eyes

Se lo agarraron de bajada porque es un cuatro ojos.

They made fun of him because he's a four-eyes.

dos caras, m, f

hypocrite/two-face, lit. two faces

Esa muchacha no es de fiar; es una dos caras.

You shouldn't trust that girl; she's such a two-face.

estar de pelos

to be really cool, lit. to be of hairs

¡Este coche está de pelos!

This car is very cool!

(estar) de peluche

(to be) cool, lit. (to be) plush

Mi vecino se compró una bicicleta de peluche.

My neighbor bought himself a very cool bike.

(estar) de puta madre

(to be) f**king great, lit. (to be) of the prostitute mother

¡Mi tío tiene un coche de puta madre!

My uncle has a f**king great car!

farol, farola

liar, hypocrite, lit. street lamp

Ese chavo es guapísimo, pero no le creas nada; es bien farol.

That guy is really hot, but don't trust him too much; he is such a liar.

fregón, fregona

top, best, lit. somebody who rubs something

Mi hermanita es muy fregona en la escuela; es la mejor de su clase.

My little sister kicks ass at school; she's top of her class.

gacho, gacha (Mexico)

meanie, lit. crooked/bent over

¡Me quitaste a mi novia, qué gacho eres!

You took away my girlfriend, what a meanie!

geniudo, geniuda

sourpuss, lit. big genius

Ese tipo nunca quiere hablar con nadie; es un geniudo.

That guy never wants to talk to anybody; he's a sourpuss.

gorrón, m
sponge, lit. big hat
Nunca compra comida para su casa; siempre anda de gorrón en otras partes.
He never buys food for his house; he's such a sponge.

hijo de la chingada
son of a bitch, lit. son of the chingada
Ese profesor es un hijo de la chingada; nos reprobó a todos.
The teacher is a son of a bitch; he failed us all.

Other variations (Mexico):
hijo de la guayaba, lit. son of the guava
hijo de la tostada, lit. son of the toast
hijo de su pelona, lit. son of his bold mother
hijo de la tiznada, lit. son of the burnt one
hijo de la trompada, lit. son of the slap on the face
hijo de su puta madre, lit. son of his prostitute mother

hinchahuevos (hinchagüevos)
pest, lit. someone who makes one's balls swell
Ahí viene otra vez este hinchagüevos; pero esta vez no le voy a abrir la puerta.
Here that pest again, but this time I'm not opening the door.

mala onda, f
mean, lit. bad wave
¡Qué mala onda! Le contaste a mi papá que saqué dinero de su cartera.
How mean! You told my dad I took money out of his wallet without asking.

35

malinchista, m, f (Mexico)

Mexican who prefers things from abroad, from *La Malinche*

Carlos es tan malinchista, que sólo ve películas gringas.

Carlos is such a lover of foreign things that he only watches American movies.

La Malinche was an American Indian woman who was the first to translate the texts of the *conquistador* Hernán Cortés. As a result, the word is used to describe people who like foreign things.

mamón, mamona (Mexico)

goody-two-shoes, lit. someone who is breastfed

Esa muchacha nunca quiere salir conmigo; es una mamona.

That girl never wants to go out with me; she's a goody-two-shoes.

mantenido, mantenida

kept man/woman, lit. maintained

José nunca ha trabajado en su vida; es un mantenido.

José has never worked in his life! He is a kept man.

mocoso, mocosa

brat, lit. full of snot

Esos mocosos me rompieron la ventana del coche con su pelota.

Those brats broke my car windshield with their ball.

mula, f

mean, lit. mule

Es bien mula con sus hijos; nunca los saca a jugar.

He's very mean to his kids; he never takes them out to play.

pendejo, pendeja

jerk, lit. pubic hair

¿Cómo dejaste salir al perro en plena ciudad? ¡Eres una pendeja!

How could you let the dog out in the city? You are such a jerk!

plato, m (Chile)

hoot, lit. plate

Mi primo se sabe los mejores chistes del mundo; ¡el chico es un plato!

My cousin knows all the jokes in the world; the dude's a hoot!

pesada, f

unbearable, lit. heavy

¡Desde que se compró un Porsche la tipa se volvió una pesada!

Since she bought herself a Porsche, she has become unbearable!

picudo, picuda

important, lit. pointy

El papá de Paco es bien picudo; trabaja con el presidente.

Paco's father is very important; he works with the president.

37

sangrón, sangrona

uptight, lit. someone who bleeds a lot

No le gusta juntarse con los de la clase. Es un sangrón.

He doesn't like to be friends with the people from the class.
He is very uptight.

sin onda

all alone, with nothing to do, lit. without a wave

Se fueron todos de vacaciones y me dejaron sin onda.

Everybody took off on vacation and they left me all alone.

tarugo, m

dumb/stupid, lit. lump of wood

¡Eres un tarugo! Te dije que no abrieras la boca.

You're so stupid! I told you not to open your mouth.

tener cara de huele-pedos

to look pissed, lit. hold a face of smell-farts

Esa señora tiene cara de huele-pedos.

That lady always looks pissed.

tener cara de pocos amigos

to look angry/annoyed, lit. to have a face of few friends

Algo te pasa esta mañana; tienes cara de pocos amigos.

Something is wrong with you this morning; you look really
annoyed.

zoquete

blockhead

El hermanito de mi novia es un zoquete.

My girlfriend's little brother is a real blockhead.

CHAPTER SIX

A patín:
Out and About, Biding One's Time

Welcome to nowhere. . . . From the busy streets of Barcelona to the Mexican Sonora Desert to the lush Andes mountains of Peru, Spanish-speaking lands feature every type of scenery you could imagine. If, while visiting the spectacular *campo,* you miss an exit or make a wrong turn, you may find yourself lost, without a friendly *amigo* in sight to give you directions. What do Hispanics call those very nice but also very distant places? Take advantage of your mistake to learn some interesting colloquial expressions. Getting lost in a foreign country may not make you a native speaker, but you'll sound like a native when sharing your misadventures with your friends back home.

As in earlier chapters, we find once again that religion has inspired many popular expressions. "As far as hell" can be translated as *donde el diablo perdió el poncho,* "where the devil lost his poncho"; e*n casa del demonio,* in the house of the devil; or *en el quinto infierno,* "in the fifth hell." At least try not to lose your soul there.

¡aguas!
watch out!, lit. waters
¡Aguas! No vayas a pisar la caca de perro.
Watch out! Don't step on that dog shit.

agarrar como al Tigre de Santa Julia
to catch someone off-guard, lit. to catch someone like the
  Tiger of Santa Julia
**Estaba haciendo pipí en el bosque cuando le cayó la
  policía y lo agarraron como al tigre de Santa Julia.**
*He was peeing in the woods when he was caught off-guard by
  the police.*

The Tiger of Santa Julia was a sort of Mexican Robin
Hood bandit of the 1920s who would steal from the rich
to give to the poor. According to legend, José de Jesús
Negrete Medina, known as *El Tigre*, died in a very unusual
manner: sitting on the toilet.

According to a review of the 2002 movie *El Tigre de
Santa Julia*, *El Tigre* lived in the town of Santa Julia, a
village that would later become part of Mexico City. Tired
of army and police corruption, *El Tigre* took justice into
his own hands; hence his nickname. And we can imagine,
based on the way he died, that *El Tigre* certainly didn't
take any shit.

a golpe de alpargata (Spain)
to walk, lit. at the bang of an espadrille
Llegamos a la escuela a golpe de alpargata.
We walked to school.

a golpe de calcetín

to walk/to go on foot, lit. at the bang of a sock

Como no servía el elevador, subimos los diez pisos a golpe de calcetín.

Since the elevator wasn't working we went up the ten floors on foot.

a las vivas

to be aware/vigilant, lit. to the live ones

Hay que andarse a las vivas, porque en el metro hay mucho ratero.

You have to be vigilant when you ride the subway—there's a lot of robbery.

a leguas

miles away

A leguas se nota que no eres de aquí.

One can tell from miles away that you are not from around here.

a los pedos

fast/speeding, lit. to the farts

Nos paró la policía porque la verdad íbamos a los pedos.

The cops stopped us because we were driving really fast.

a todo trapo/mecha/máquina

quickly, lit. to the whole cloth/wick/machine

Enrique salió de su casa a todo trapo, y aun así perdió el autobús.

Enrique left his house quickly but he missed the bus anyway.

al tiro (Chile)
immediately, lit. to the shot
¡Le pidió matrimonio y ella le dijo que sí al tiro!
He asked her to marry him and she accepted immediately!

andar a patín
to walk / to go on foot, lit. to skate
Mi papá me quitó el coche y ahora ando siempre a patín.
My dad took my car away, and now I always walk.

cacharro, m
lemon (car), lit. pots and pans
Mi coche es un cacharro inútil.
My car is a real lemon.

dejada, f (Mexico)
cab ride/trip, lit. left
**A partir de las diez, los taxistas cobran cincuenta
   pesos extra por dejada.**
*Starting at ten o'clock, the cabbies charge a fifty peso per trip
   surcharge.*

de un jalón
in one go, lit. of one pull
Vamos a pintar la casa de un jalón.
Let's paint the house in one go.

de uvas a peras (Spain)
once in a blue moon, rarely, lit. from grapes to pears
**Mi hermano vive cerca de aquí, pero lo vemos de uvas
   a peras.**
*My brother lives nearby, but we only see him once in a blue
   moon.*

Language is never short of words to describe those long periods of time without seeing a friend or family member or having a special event. There's some note of impatience in those expressions, meaning "rarely in a lifetime." *De higos a brevas,* from figs to early figs, is a natural time, almost one year from the last figs to the first ones. *A cada muerte de Obispo,* "at each bishop's death," refers to the long period a bishop stays in his post. It seems they don't want to retire and once they're appointed bishop they intend to die a bishop too. The Catholic calendar inspired *cada día de San Juan,* "not so often," since a saint's day happens only once a year. The expression *de Pascuas a Ramos,* "from Easter to Palm Sunday," suggests a time span of a bit less than one year.

donde el indio perdió el huarache
in the middle of nowhere, lit. where the Indian lost his huarache (sandal)
La casa de Tomás está muy lejos; allá donde el indio perdió el huarache.
Tomás's house is really far away; he lives in the middle of nowhere.

el año de la pera (Chile)
long time ago, lit. year of the pear
Esa canción es buenísima, pero es del año de la pera.
That song is really good, but it's very old.

When was it exactly? Facing your new antiques purchase or visiting a old folks' home, you can now date everything and everyone from *el año del caldo,* "the year of the broth"; *el año del cocol* (Mexico), "the year of the *cocol*" (a type of bread); *el año de la canica,* "the year of the marble"; *el año de la cachetada,* "the year of the smack in the face" (that parents shouldn't celebrate too often); *el año de la nana,* "the year of the grandmother" (that should last forever); *el año de Mari Castaña,* "the year of the Mari Castaña" (go check this one out online); and finally, *el año de la sopa,* "the year of the soup." The main advantage of this system is that, as the exact beginning and ending dates of the periods are not given, you can use it without worrying about people or things that have passed a certain age. . . .

en dos patadas
really fast (in a New York minute), lit. in two kicks
Terminamos la tarea en dos patadas
We finished the homework really fast.

en la concha del mundo
in bum-f**k Egypt, lit. in the vagina of the world
Vamos a juntarnos mejor en mi casa; Carlos vive en la concha del mundo.
Let's meet at my place instead; you know Carlos lives in bum-f**k Egypt.

en un abrir y cerrar de ojos

in the blink of an eye, lit. in an open and close of the eyes

Me di la vuelta, y en un abrir y cerrar de ojos desapareció la mujer con la que había estado hablando.

I turned around, and in the blink of an eye the lady I had been talking to vanished.

en un dos por tres

in a New York minute, lit. in a two-by-three

No te preocupes; te preparo algo de comer en un dos por tres.

Don't worry, I'll fix you something to eat in a New York minute.

hacer dedo

to thumb a ride, lit. to make finger

El coche se nos descompuso en medio de la nada, así que tuvimos que hacer dedo.

The car broke down in the middle of nowhere, so we had to thumb a ride.

hacerla cansada

to take one's time, lit. to make it tired

La banda salió hasta las once; los organizadores del concierto la hicieron muy cansada.

The band came out at eleven; the concert organizers really took their time.

hecho/hecha la mocha

very fast, lit. made the *mocha* (an incomplete train)

Me encontré a Marina esta mañana, pero no platicamos mucho porque iba hecha la mocha.

I found Marina this morning, but we didn't chat much because she was going really fast.

judío errante, m
vagabond, lit. wandering Jew
A Inés nunca le gustó establecerse; le gusta la vida de judío errante.
Inés never wanted to settle down; she likes the life of a vagabond.

nave, f
car, lit. shuttle
Me encanta tu nave, ¿cuánto te costó?
I love your car; how much did you pay for it?

norteado, norteada
lost/disoriented, lit. "northerned"/stuck in the North
Vamos a preguntarle al policía cómo llegar; yo estoy muy norteado.
Let's ask the cop how to get there; I'm lost.

¡ojo!
watch out!, lit. eye
¡Ojo! Esa avenida es muy peligrosa.
Watch out! This avenue is very dangerous.

pedir aventón
to ask for a ride, lit. to ask for a push
Vamos a pedir aventón; ya me canso de caminar.
Let's ask for a ride; I am tired of walking.

una vuelta a la manzana
around the block, lit. a lap of the apple
Anoche, me llevé al perro a dar una vuelta a la manzana.
Last night I took the dog for a walk around the block.

CHAPTER SEVEN

A falta de pan, tortillas:
Food, Glorious Food

Good news for night owls visiting Spain: unless you skip dinner, you won't be in bed until midnight, as Spain follows a very relaxed meal plan that lasts well into the evening. Lunch is traditionally served between two and four, while dinner is held from ten to midnight. Don't bother with an early-bird special, as no self-respecting Spanish restaurant opens its doors before seven! Mexico and many other parts of Latin America have retained this aspect of Spanish culture and eat quite late. Families eat together and meals are not taken lightly (no pun intended).

A famous Spanish delicacy is *jamón serrano*—you'll see enormous hams hanging from every delicatessen. In Peru, Bolivia, and Ecuador, however, forget the ham . . . and say hello to the guinea pig. That cuddly albeit whiny pet *gringo* kids love is the favorite dinner of many a Latin American youngster. *Cuy,* the national dish of Peru, is succulent guinea pig roasted with herbs. And no, it doesn't taste like chicken, but has a unique chewy, gamey taste all its own. If hunger strikes between meals in Mexico, have no fear. Visit one of the many street vendors who sell crispy *chapulines*—fried grasshoppers—or stop by for a *quesadilla de sesos,* brain quesadilla; *taco de lengua,* tongue taco; or a *pancita picante,* spicy stomach. Rather than making a guest appearance on *Fear Factor,* you can travel to Latin America and sample all kinds of strange food.

a falta de pan, tortillas

half a loaf is better than none, lit. if there's no bread, tortillas

Como la chica no quiso salir conmigo, invité mejor a su prima; ¡a falta de pan, tortillas!

Since the girl I liked didn't want to go out with me, I invited her cousin instead. Half a loaf is better than none!

a partir un piñón

two peas in a pod, lit. to split up a pine nut

Parece que son muy buenos amigos; están a partir un piñón.

It looks like they are very good friends—two peas in a pod.

comer camote

to fail to pay attention, lit. to eat sweet potato

Los chicos no se movieron cuando les dije; estaban comiendo camote.

The kids didn't move when I told them to because they weren't paying attention.

comer como pelón de hospicio

to eat like there's no tomorrow, lit. to eat like a bold child from an orphanage

Mi sobrino come como pelón de hospicio.

My nephew eats like there's no tomorrow.

comer el mandado

to beat someone to something, lit. to eat the groceries

Justo cuando Raúl se iba a declarar a la chica nueva, otro tipo le comió el mandado.

Just when Raúl was about to declare his love to the new girl at school, another guy beat him to it.

comiendo moras

to be distracted, lit. eating berries

Le dije al mecánico que me iba a echar en reversa, pero estaba comiendo moras y no se movió.

I told the mechanic I was backing up, but he was really distracted and didn't move out of the way.

cachar a alguien con las manos en la masa

to catch somebody red-handed, lit. to catch somebody with his or her hands on the dough

Estaba en la cocina besando a la muchacha, y mi mamá nos cachó con las manos en la masa.

I was in the kitchen kissing the maid, and my mom caught us red-handed.

crema y nata, f

cream of society, lit. cream and heavy cream

La cena estuvo increíble; llegó la crema y nata de México.

The dinner was fantastic; the cream of Mexican society was there.

darle a alguien chicharrón

to kill someone or something, lit. to give someone chitlins

Los perros le dieron chicharrón a las gallinas.

The dogs killed the hens.

dar atole con el dedo

to lie/to swindle/to cheat, lit. to give thick warm milk (atole)
with the finger

**El presidente Fox dijo mucho y no hizo nada; nomás nos
dio atole con el dedo.**

President Fox talked a lot and did nothing; he just lied to us.

de chile, dulce y manteca

to run the gamut, lit. of chili, sweets, and lard

**En la fiesta de Carlota había gente de todas partes;
de chile, dulce y manteca.**

*At Carlota's party there were all kinds of people; they ran
the gamut.*

echar la sal

to jinx something/wish bad things on, lit. to throw salt on

**Mi hermano me dijo que me iba ir mal en el examen
sólo para echarme la sal.**

My brother told me I would fail the exam just to jinx me.

el negrito en el arroz

the negative side of the story, lit. the little black one in the
bowl of rice

**Los periodistas nunca hablan bien del gobierno; siem-
pre están buscando el negrito en el arroz.**

*Journalists never say good things about the government; they
are always looking for the negative side of the story.*

en todas partes se cuecen habas

it only takes one, lit. everywhere one cooks broad beans

**Son ricos pero el hijo salió criminal; en todas partes se
cuecen habas.**

They are rich but the son was a dirty criminal; it only takes one.

empacar

to eat, lit. to pack

Vayan empacando porque nos tenemos que ir pronto.

Start eating now, because we have to leave soon.

galleta, f

slap in the face, lit. cookie

El niño lloraba pidiendoun heldo, pero la madre le metió una galleta.

The kid cried for an ice cream, but his mother slapped him instead.

Lit. The kid cried for an ice cream, but his mother gave him a cookie instead.

hacer de chivo los tamales

to cheat/swindle someone, lit. to make young goat tamales

Ese software no sirve para nada; la vendedora nos hizo de chivo los tamales.

That software is good for nothing; we fell for the saleswoman's sweet-talk.

hasta en la sopa

to be everywhere, lit. even in the soup

Esta actriz aparece hasta en la sopa; su cara está en la portada de todas las revistas.

This actress appears everywhere—her face is on the cover of every magazine.

harina de otro costal

another can of worms, lit. flour from another sack

No mezcles tu vida personal con la escuela; eso es harina de otro costal.

Don't mix your personal life with school; that's another can of worms.

hincar el diente

to take a bite of, lit. to cram the teeth

Como quisiera hincarle el diente a ese pastel.

How I wish I could take a bite of that cake.

manzana de la discordia, f

bone of contention, lit. apple of contention

**La herencia de la abuela fue la manzana de la discordia
entre nosotros, los nietos.**

*Grandma's inheritance became a bone of contention among us
grandchildren.*

¡mangos!

no way, lit. mangos

**Mi ex novio dijo que lo recogiera en el aeropuerto, pero
¡ni mangos!**

*My ex-boyfriend asked me to pick him up at the airport, but
there's no way I'd do that!*

mezclar peras con manzanas

to mix apples and oranges, lit. to mix pears with apples

**Estamos hablando de tu tarea y no de la mia; no mezcles
peras con manzanas.**

*We're talking about your homework here, and not mine; don't
mix apples and oranges.*

moros con cristianos

rice and beans, lit. Moors with Christians

**Me fascina la comida cubana; sobre todo los moros con
cristianos.**

I love Cuban food! Especially rice and beans.

mover el bigote

to eat, lit. to move the mustache

A mi abuela le encanta mover el bigote.

My grandma loves to eat.

mucho ruido y pocas nueces

much ado about nothing, lit. a lot of noise, but very few nuts

Esa película de acción es mucho ruido y pocas nueces.

That action movie is much ado about nothing.

ni torta

not a thing, lit. not a cake/sandwich

¡Bájale a tu música – no oigo ni torta!

Turn down your music—I can't hear a thing!

It's not enough to know that *torta* is a sandwich in Mexico; once you start moving about the continent, things get trickier. *Torta* has dozens of meanings elsewhere besides "cake"; a *torta* in Spain can mean "a slap in the face": *Me dijo una grosería y le di una torta* means "He told me something nasty and I slapped his face." Looking for sympathy in Costa Rica? Tell someone your life is full of sandwiches, and they'll understand the problems you're facing. *Su vida es muy compleja y está llena de tortas* means "His life is very complicated and full of problems."

no saber ni papa

to not know jack, lit. to not know potato

Mañana nos toca examen de mate y no sé ni papa.

There is a math test tomorrow and I don't know jack.

pan comido, m
piece of cake, lit. eaten bread
**Después de todo el recorrido que hicimos en la bici,
el último kilómetro ya es pan comido.**
*After all we've biked so far, the last kilometer is going to be a
piece of cake.*

pan de todos los días, m
daily thing, lit. everyday bread
**La conferencia de prensa del alcalde es pan de todos
los días.**
The mayor's press conference is a daily thing.

pedir peras al olmo
to ask for the moon, lit. to ask the elm for pears
**La maestra me pidió que ya no llegara tarde, pero eso
es como pedirle peras al olmo.**
*The teacher asked me not to be late again, but that's like ask-
ing for the moon.*

ser plato de segunda mesa
to be second fiddle, lit. to be a plate of second table
**Como Mariana le dijo que no, me quiso llevar a mí al
baile. Pero le dije que yo no soy plato de segunda
mesa.**
*As Mariana told him no, he wanted me to go dancing with
him. But I said I was no second fiddle.*

puras habas (Mexico)
nothing/shit, lit. pure broad beans
Yo de eso sé puras habas.
I know shit about that.

servirse con la cuchara grande

to leave the best for oneself, lit. to serve oneself with the big
  spoon

**Lucio se sirvió con la cuchara grande y le sacó a le
  bailar a la hija del director.**

*Lucio saved the best for himself and invited the director's
  daughter for a dance.*

dar una sopa de su propio chocolate

to give someone a taste of their own medicine, lit. to give a
  soup of his/her own chocolate

**Después de que mi tío se portó tan mal, mi tía le dio una
  sopa de su propio chocolate.**

*After my uncle behaved badly, my aunt gave him a taste of his
  own medicine.*

sólo mis chicharrones truenan

only I count, lit. only my chitlins make noise

**Olvídate de los demás empleados; en esta oficina sólo
  mis chicharrones truenan.**

*Forget about the other employees; in this company only I
  count.*

voltear la tortilla

to turn the tables, lit. to flip the tortilla

**Puede que al principio te saliste con la tuya, pero
  ahora se volteó la tortilla y ¡vas a tener que pagar!**

*You may have gotten away with your silly game the first time,
  but now the tables have turned and you're going to pay
  for it!*

CHAPTER EIGHT

Como cosacos:

Beer Before Liquor . . .

Any visit to a Spanish-speaking country will provide you with all the delicious alcoholic beverages you may need. The French and Italians may be known for their wine, but Spain, Mexico, and Cuba have an abundance of other alcoholic drinks to wet your whistle. Spanish specialties include *jerez,* from the Andalusian town of Jeréz, and *cava,* a local sparkling wine. Looking for something stronger? Head across the Atlantic and stop off in Cuba for a tasty *cuba libre*—spicy dark rum, Coca-Cola, and lime. Among Cuban exiles, they're known as *mentiritas,* little lies.

Still thirsty? Mosey on down to Mexico and indulge in the national drink, *tequila.* Made from the *agave* plant, *tequila* is best drunk shot-style after a lick of salt followed by a dose of lime, in a *margarita,* or if you're lucky enough to get the high-quality stuff, sipped slowly over ice. No worm in your *tequila* bottle? No worries, there shouldn't be, although *mezcal,* a sister beverage made from the *agave* as well, may contain a worm. Nowadays, nearly all worms are raised specifically to add to bottles of *mezcal* or *tequila* for the sheer delight/disgust of *gringos.*

ahogado, ahogada
plastered, lit. drawn
Carlos y sus amigos andan ahogados otra vez.
Carlos and his friends are plastered again.

a palo seco
straight, lit. at dry stick
No sé cómo pueden tomar todo ese tequila a palo seco.
I don't know how you can drink all that tequila straight.

beber como una esponja
to drink like a fish, lit. to drink like a sponge
**Mis amigos de la universidad son muy divertidos;
     beben como una esponja.**
My friends from university are a lot of fun; they drink like fish.

beber como cosacos
to drink like a fish, lit. to drink like a Cossack
**Cuando terminen las clases nos vamos a ir a beber
     como cosacos.**
As soon as the classes are over, we'll go drink like fish.

caballito, m (Mexico)
shot, lit. little horse
Vamos a echarnos un caballito de tequila.
Let's have a shot of tequila.

estar como una cuba
to be very drunk, lit. to be like a bucket
**Nos acabamos la botella de vodka y nos pusimos como
     una cuba.**
We drank the whole bottle of vodka and ended up very drunk.

chela, cheve, f (Mexico)
beer
Vámonos a echar una chela.
Let's go and have a beer.

chupar
to drink, lit. to suck
Los mexicanos saben chupar.
Mexicans know how to drink.

cruda, f (Mexico)
hangover, lit. raw
Tómense un antiácido para evitar la cruda.
Take an antacid to avoid a hangover.

caña, f (Chile)
hangover, lit. sugar cane
No me puedo levantar con la tremenda caña que traigo.
I can't get up with this awful hangover.

caña, f (Spain)
drink, lit. sugar cane
Vamos a echarnos una caña después del trabajo.
Let's go out for a drink after work.

dormir la mona
to sleep it off, lit. to sleep the female monkey
**Con la borrachera que se puso anoche, Diana se pasó
todo el día durmiendo la mona.**
*Diana was so drunk last night that she spent all day sleeping
it off.*
*lit. With the drunkenness she had last night, Diana spent all
day sleeping the monkey.*

empinar el codo
to drink / to knock them back, lit. to bend the elbow
Tan temprano y ya están empinando el codo?
It's so early and you're already knocking them back?

Drunken revelry can be either funny or sad, depending on the point of view. Even if boozehounds may speak during their drunkenness, most of the expressions associated with this state are the work of sober observers. Some expressions refer to a drunkard's change in personality. While some drinkers will start acting stupid, the Spanish use *estar burro*, to be drunk, "to be donkey." Yet others will speak quickly and make a lot of noise, hence *estar cuete (cohete)/ponerse un cuete*, "to be/become a rocket."

Drinking is not a science, but some people learn when to stop. As standing up straight can be a challenge, this fight between balance and gravity is referred to in *estar hasta atrás*, "to be all the way at the back"—one more shot and the drinker will fall flat on his or her face! Other expressions include *estar hasta aquí*, "to be up to here"; *estar hasta las manitas*, "to be up to the little hands"; *estar hasta el gorro*, "to be up to the hat"; and *estar hasta la madre*, "to be up to the mother." In the same spirit but a little bit more vulgar is *estar hasta el culo*, "to be up to the ass."

When facing a drunk, Chileans may say that the person *está curado*, "is cured." Well, every medicine may have some side effects and the *cruda*—the hangover waiting around the corner—will teach him a lesson!

estar en pedo (Argentina) / estar pedo (Mexico)
to be very drunk, lit. to be in a fart, to be fart
Mi compañero de cuarto estaba en pedo y terminó anoche en mi cama.
My roommate was so drunk that he ended up in my bed last night!

estar jarra
to be drunk, lit. to be jar
Yo ya estaba muy jarra cuando me subí a la barra a bailar.
I was pretty drunk when I climbed up on the bar to dance.

estar mamado (Spain)
to be dead drunk, lit. to be breastfed
Jacinto no puede ni levantarse; está muy mamado.
Jacinto cannot even get up; he's dead drunk.

estar hasta las manitas
to be drunk, lit. to be up to the little hands
El portero de la escuela siempre está hasta las manitas.
The school doorman is always very drunk.

goma, f (Mexico)
hangover, lit. rubber
Jerome no puede moverse de la goma que trae.
Jerome is so hung-over that he can barely move.

hacer equis
to walk like a drunk, lit. to make Xs on the ground
Caminan haciendo equis.
They walk like drunks.

la del estribo
one for the road, lit. that of the stirrup
Vamos a echarnos la del estribo y luego nos vamos.
Let's have one for the road and leave after that.

pasársele a alguien las cucharadas
to be wasted, lit. to be over spoonfuls
**Mejor llévate a tu prima a su casa; ya se le pasaron las
cucharadas.**
Better take your cousin home; she's already wasted.

pomo, m
booze, lit. bottle, pharmacy
**Ya tenemos todo para la cena; sólo falta comprar el
pomo.**
Everything is ready for dinner; we just need to buy the booze.

fría, f
beer, lit. cold one
Hace tanto calor que me voy a tomar una fría.
It's so hot that I'll have a beer.

CHAPTER 9

Arrastrando la cobija:
Feelings and Emotions

With spicy Latino blood running through their veins, many Hispanic *hombres* will not be keen to share with you the feelings and emotions in this chapter. If there's one thing these men have mastered, it's *machismo*. Originally a Spanish word, it has been adopted by languages across the globe to define super masculine behavior and attitude. A true cult of virility, *machismo* draws on two basic principles, aggression and sexuality. Men must show they are powerful and protect women, while also boasting sexual prowess. This has had lasting effects not only on Latinas, but on Latino men themselves.

On the other hand, *machismo* has been decreasing in Spain for the past twenty years, perhaps because the country's prominent rise through EU membership from a sleepy monarchy to an economic powerhouse. Either that, or the virility is wearing off . . . Spain has one of the lowest birth rates in Europe. In Latin America the birthrate has decreased significantly; in the 1960s, Latin American women had, on average, 6 children, but today they still have an average of 2.7 children in their lifetimes.

llorar a moco tendido

to cry inconsolably, lit. to cry with snot hanging

Se la pasó toda la película llorando a moco tendido.

She spent the entire movie crying inconsolably.

andar arrastrando la cobija

to be sad/depressed, lit. to be dragging the bedsheet

¡Pobre! Desde que lo dejó su novia anda arrastrando la cobija.

Poor guy! Since his girlfriend left him, he's been very depressed.

a los cuatro vientos

for everyone to see/hear, lit. to the four winds

La feliz pareja salió a gritar su amor a los cuatro vientos.

The happy couple has declared their love to everyone who will listen.

a chaleco

forcefully, lit. at the vest

Le van a sacar la información a chaleco.

They are going to get the information out of him whether he likes it or not.

a huevo

by force, lit. at the egg

Yo sé que no me quiere decir nada, pero le voy a sacar la información a huevo.

I know she doesn't want to tell me anything, but I will get the information out of her by force.

andar con pies de plomo

to be very careful/cautious, lit. to walk with lead feet

Si no quieres hacerle daño a Julia, más te vale que te andes con pies de plomo.

If you don't want to hurt Julia's feelings, you'd better be careful about what you say.

andarse por las ramas

to beat around the bush, lit. to wander among the tree branches

Ese chico nunca dice las cosas como son; siempre se anda por las ramas.

Jasper never tells the truth when first asked; he's always beating around the bush.

a capa y espada

to defend something or someone at all cost, lit. with a cape and a sword

Defendió a su marido a capa y espada.

She defended her husband at all cost.

a calzón quitado

to the point, lit. with the underwear off

A mí me gusta decir las cosas como son: siempre a calzón quitado.

I like to say things the way they are—I get right to the point.

ahogarse en un vaso de agua

to make a fuss out of nothing, lit. to drown in a glass of water

Tu problema tiene una solución fácil; no te ahogues en un vaso de agua.

Your problem has an easy solution; don't make a big fuss out of nothing.

arriesgar el cuero

to risk one's life, lit. to risk one's flesh

Los inmigrantes arriesgaron el cuero, pero por fin llegaron a los Estados Unidos.

The immigrants risked their lives, but finally made it to the United States.

caer de la gracia

to fall out of someone's favor, lit. to fall from grace

Esos muchachos de la cuadra son tan ruidosos que ya cayeron de mi gracia.

Those kids from the block are so noisy, I can't stand them anymore.

caer redondito

to fall for something, lit. to fall round

Le dije de broma que se había sacado la lotería y ¡cayó redondito!

I told him jokingly that he'd hit the jackpot and he fell for it!

caer como balde de agua fría

to come as a shock, lit. as a cold water bucket

Su carta de despedida me cayó como balde de agua fría.

Her farewell letter hit me like a ton of bricks.

campechano, campechana

relaxed, unfazed, lit. somebody from Campeche (a Mexican state)

Las ratas se paseaban muy campechanas por ahí, aunque el gato andaba cerca.

The rats were walking about unfazed by the cat hiding nearby.

circularle atole por las venas

heart of stone, lit. to have thick milk running through the veins

Nunca se conmueve con nada; parece que le corre atole por las venas.

He never seems to be moved by anything; it seems he has a heart of stone.

como Dios le da a entender

to improvise, lit. as God made him or her understand

Nunca he sido muy bueno en el karaoke, pero ayer canté como Dios me dio a entender y al público le fascinó.

I'm not very good at karaoke, but I improvised a great song last night and people loved it!

con el alma en un hilo

to be worried sick, lit. with the soul hanging from a thread

Como no llegaste a trabajar ayer, nos tenías con el alma en un hilo.

When you didn't show up at work yesterday, we were worried sick about you.

con el corazón en la boca

to be worried, lit. with the heart in the mouth

Las niñas se fueron solas y me tenían con el corazón en la boca.

The girls left by themselves and they had me worried sick.

con el Jesús en la boca

to be anxious/worried, lit. with Jesus in the mouth

¿Por qué no llamaste antes? Me tenías con el Jesús en la boca.

Why didn't you call earlier? I was worried about you!

con el agua al cuello

up to one's neck, lit. with the water up to the neck

Mi tía se quedó sin trabajo y las deudas la tienen con el agua al cuello.

My aunt lost her job and is buried up to her neck in debt.

con la cola entre las patas

with one's tail between his or her legs

Hernán regresó con la cola entre las patas a pedirle perdón a Maya.

Hernán came back with his tail between his legs and asked for Maya's forgiveness.

estar como agua para chocolate

to be in a very nasty mood, lit. like water for chocolate

Desde que la dejó el marido, la cocinera está como agua para chocolate.

Since her husband left her, the cook has been in a really nasty mood.

ser chino libre

to be free, lit. to be a free Chinese person

Ahora que se fueron mis papás de viaje, soy china libre.

With my parents away on vacation, I am finally free.

chiflando en la loma

to be left hanging, lit. whistling in the mountain

La novia de Ricardo se fue con otro y lo dejó chiflando en la loma.

Ricardo's girlfriend took off with another guy and left him hanging.

darse por bien servido

to receive something undeserved, lit. to consider oneself
well-served

Le dimos lo que se pudo; que se dé por bien servido.
*We gave the officer what we could; he should consider him-
self well-served.*

darse color

to realize, lit. to give oneself color

No me había dado color de que estabas parado allí.
I hadn't realized you were standing there.

de capa caída

depressed/down, lit. of fallen cape

Desde que Oscar perdió el trabajo, anda de capa caída.
Since Oscar lost his job, he's been down.

de a seis

astonished/surprised, lit. of a six

**Cuando mi novio me dijo que iba a cambiar de sexo, me
quedé de a seis.**
*When my boyfriend told me he was going to change sex, I
was speechless.*

de a ocho

astonished, lit. of an eight

**Cuando les dije que me iba a casar se quedaron de a
ocho.**
*When I told them I was getting married, my parents were
astonished.*

de noche
to not know shit, lit. at night
No sé ni cómo Mariana se graduó de la preparatoria; pasó la primaria de noche.
I don't know how Mariana graduated from high-school; she virtually missed primary school.

embarrarla
to make a mistake, lit. to smear it
Ya no le voy a pedir nada a tu secretaria; siempre la embarra.
I will never ask your secretary for anything; she always f**ks up.

echarse al monte
to rebel against somebody, lit. to throw oneself to the mountain
El adolescente se echó al monte cuando su mamá le dijo que no podía salir.
The teenager threw a fit when her mother told her she couldn't go out.

echarse para atrás (Latin America)
to change one's mind, lit. to throw oneself backwards
Mi papá dijo que iba a ir a mi graduación, pero después se echó para atrás.
My father said he would go to my graduation, but then he said he wouldn't.

en la olla
to be in financial trouble, lit. in the pot
Josh tiene que pagar sus deudas de estudiante, pero está en la olla.
Josh has to pay back his student loans, but he is already in financial trouble.

entre azul y buenas noches

flaky, lit. between blue and good night

Ese tipo no tiene convicciones; siempre está entre azul y buenas noches.

That guy's not very assertive; he's flaky.

traer a alguien entre ojos

to have it out for someone, lit. to have someone in between the eyes

Esa maestra ya me trae entre ojos; siempre me pregunta lo más difícil.

The teacher has it out for me; she's always asking me the tough questions.

en el hoyo

up shit's creek, lit. in the pits

No tenemos dinero y ya nos cortaron la luz; estamos en el hoyo.

We have no money and the electricity was just cut—we're up shit's creek.

entre la espada y la pared

between a rock and a hard place, lit. between the sword and the wall

La decisión que quieren que tome es muy difícil y me pone entre la espada y la pared.

The difficult decision I have to make puts me between a rock and a hard place.

enchinarse el cuero

to get goose bumps, lit. to have the skin curled up

Nada más de ver a mi novio en su uniforme de soldado se me enchina el cuero.

Seeing my boyfriend in that soldier's uniform gives me goose bumps.

en veremos

not a sure thing, lit. in we will see

Lo del viaje a México todavía está en veremos.

The trip to Mexico's still not a sure thing.

estar de mala hostia (Spain)

to be in a bad mood, lit. to be of bad host

Ni le hables por teléfono a Mariana; hoy está de mala hostia.

Don't even call Mariana on the phone; she's in a really bad mood.

estar en un lecho de rosas

to be in a very good situation, lit. to be on a bed of roses

Dices que lo estás pasando mal, pero yo no estoy en un lecho de rosas.

You say you are going through a bad time; well, I'm not doing so well myself.

hacer una tempestad en un vaso de agua

to make a fuss about something, lit. to make a storm in a glass of water

Deja de llorar; siempre haces una tempestad en un vaso de agua.

Stop crying; you're always making a tempest in a teapot.

hacer un papelón

to make a scene, lit. to make a big paper

Cuando le dije a mi novia que ya no la quería, me hizo un papelón.

When I told my girlfriend that I didn't love her anymore, she made such a scene.

hacerse bolas

to be confused, lit. to make balls of oneself

Tengo que volver a contar, pues ya me hice bolas.

I have to start counting again because I'm confused now.

hacer los mandados (a alguien)

to fail to intimidate, lit. to run errands

Puede verse muy fortachón, pero a mi ese muchacho me hace los mandados.

Justin might look really buff, but he fails to intimidate me.

lit. Justin might look really buff, but he doesn't make me run errands.

hacerse como quien oye llover

to pretend not to hear something, lit. like someone hearing the rain

Le pregunté a mi jefe cuándo me va a subir el sueldo y se hizo como quien oye llover.

I asked my boss when I'll get a raise, but he pretended not to hear.

las duras y las maduras

thick and thin, lit. the hard ones and the mature ones

Pasé las duras y las maduras, pero al fin conseguí una entrevista.

I went through thick and thin to get the interview.

licuársele el hígado [a alguien]

to make someone's blood boil, lit. to liquify someone's liver

Cada vez que veo a mi ex marido, se me licúa el hígado.

Every time I see my former husband, he makes my blood boil.

lit. Every time I see my former husband, my liver liquefies.

llegarle el agua al cuello

to be in dire straits, lit. to have the water up to the neck

**Ojalá que ya encuentre trabajo, porque le está llegando
    el agua al cuello.**

I hope he can find a job soon; he's in dire straits.

lloverle en su milpita

to have a streak of bad luck, lit. to rain on one's land (*milpa*,
    from Náhuatl *milli*)

**¡Pobre Miguel! Lo dejó la mujer y lo echaron del tra-
    bajo, ahora sí le llovió en su milpita.**

*Poor Miguel, he was fired and his wife left him; he's had a
    streak of bad luck.*

meter un calambre

to put a scare, lit. to put a cramp

La policía les cayó encima y les metió un calambre.

The cops came over and put a scare on them.

no estar el horno para bollos

to not be in the mood, lit. to not have the oven ready for bread

**Ni le hables a mi mamá de tus calificaciones, porque
    no está el horno para bollos.**

*Don't even mention your grades to Mom. She's clearly not in
    the mood.*

no quitar el dedo del renglón

to persist / to not give up, lit. to not take the finger off the line

Conseguir el trabajo no es fácil, pero no voy a quitar el dedo del renglón.

Getting the job won't be easy, but I will not give up.

pasar las de Caín

to go through hell and high water, lit. to go through what Cain went through

Para conseguir una greencard, Jackie tuvo que pasar las de Caín.

Jackie had to go through hell and high water to get a green card.

pedir esquina

to have enough, lit. to ask for corner

¡Ya pido esquina! No veo para cuando terminar la tesis.

I've had enough! I don't know when I will finish the thesis.

perder los estribos

to lose one's temper, lit. to lose the stirrups

No le digas nada a Mariana porque ya está a punto de perder los estribos.

Don't tell Mariana anything because she's already on the verge of losing her temper.

poner el grito en el cielo

to protest/complain, lit. to put the scream in heaven

Cuando le dije que iba a renunciar, mi jefe puso el grito en el cielo.

When I told him I was quitting, my boss protested loudly.

ponerse el saco

to incriminated oneself, lit. to put on the jacket

Nadie le dijo a Gerry que él estaba involucrado pero él mismo se puso el saco.

Nobody said Gerry was involved, but he incriminated himself.

ponerse los moños

to play hard to get, lit. to put ribbons on oneself

Invitamos a salir a Patricia, pero como siempre se puso sus moños.

We asked Patricia to go out with us but as always she played hard to get.

quedar bien

to behave, lit. to stay well

Después del escándalo de anoche, Tomás está haciendo todo lo posible por quedar bien.

After last night's scandal, Tomás is going out of his way to behave.

quemárseles las habas [a alguien]

to be anxious, lit. to burn one's broad beans

¡Qué bueno que llegaste! Se me queman las habas por contarte el último chisme.

I'm so glad you're here! I can't wait to give you all the latest gossip.

quitarse la espina

to get something off one's chest, lit. to take out the thorn

Te voy a decir el secreto, pero sólo para quitarme la espina.

I will tell you my secret, but only to just to get it off my chest.

rajarse

to chicken / wimp out, lit. to scratch oneself

¡No te rajes! Échate la otra . . .

Don't wimp out, have another drink . . .

regarla

to make a mistake, lit. to water it

¡Ya la regamos! Nos pasamos la salida.

We screwed it up! We missed the exit.

sacar el cobre

to show one's true colors, lit. to take out the copper

Al principio, George era muy amable con todos, pero luego sacó el cobre.

At the beginning George was nice to everybody, but soon he showed his true colors.

saco de pulgas, m

nervous, antsy, lit. fleabag

¡Tranquilízate! Hoy estás como un saco de pulgas.

Relax! You're really antsy today.

sacar de quicio, m

to drive somebody crazy, lit. to take out of the (door) jam

La falta de educación de mi jefe realmente me saca de quicio.

My boss's lack of education really drives me crazy.

volando bajo

to be low, down, lit. flying low

No sé qué le pasa, pero Curtis lleva días volando bajo.

I don't know what's wrong with Curtis, but he has been pretty low lately.

CHAPTER TEN

El oro y el moro:
Breaking the Bank

The legend of El Dorado, a land supposedly teaming with gold and precious stones, began in present-day Colombia. A tribal chief would cover his body in gold dust and dive into a pure mountain lake. Rumors of this ritual spread, and soon Spanish conquistadors in South America began their quest to find the source of such riches. They may not have found El Dorado, but they certainly found enough gold and silver to bring wealth and prosperity to the Spanish monarchy and indirectly to the Catholic Church.

andar pato (Chile)
to be broke, lit. to walk duck
No invites a Rodrigo a salir con nosotros; siempre anda bien pato.
Don't even ask Rodrigo to come out with us; he's always broke.

andar bruja (Mexico)
to be broke, lit. to go witch
No puedo pagar la renta este mes; ando bien bruja.
I can't pay the rent this month; I am really broke.

agarrado, agarrada

stingy bastard, lit. grabbed

Mi viejo es un agarrado; no me quiso dar para ir al cine.

My old man is a stingy bastard; he didn't give me any money for the movies.

billete, m

dough, lit. bill

Desde que Jorge trabaja en el gobierno, se mete el puro billete.

Since Jorge started working with the government, he makes a lot of dough.

chafa, f

fake, lit. to ruin

Esa chaqueta está tan barata que seguro es chafa

That jacket is so cheap that I'm sure it's fake.

codo, m

stingy, lit. elbow

¡Qué codo! Ganaste ayer en el hipódromo y no nos invitas ni una chela.

How stingy! You won last night at the track and you won't even buy us a beer.

disparar

to be "on" someone, lit. to shoot

Vamos al cine; yo disparo las entradas.

Let's go to the movies; the tickets are on me.

disparador, disparadora

generous, lit. shooter

Cuando gana en el póker, mi papá se vuelve muy disparador.

Every time he wins at poker, my dad becomes very generous.

echar un volado

to flip a coin, lit. to throw a flown one

Vamos a echar un volado a ver quién va por el pomo.

Let's flip a coin to see who will go and get the booze.

Flipping a coin is playing Julius Caesar passing the Rubicon. His phrase *Alea jacta est* is Latin for "the die is cast," and refers to a popular Roman dice game. *Alea,* meaning "dice," gave birth to the Spanish word for random, *aleatorio.* Once the coin is in the air, the outcome is purely random. Whereas Americans play heads or tails, Mexicans call *águila o sol,* eagle or sun, from the two faces of their national coins. Before the arrival of the euro, Spanish coins had a face on one side and a cross on the other. As a result, heads or tails in Spain is called *cara o cruz,* face or cross. The same principle in Colombia inspired *cara o sello,* face or seal. Even if you suffer from bad luck at this game, at least you'll have learned some new expressions.

caerse con la lana (Mexico)

to cough up the dough, lit. to fall down with the wool

Le tuve que pedir prestado a mi novia, pues mi mamá no se cayó con la lana.

I had to borrow money from my girlfriend because my mom didn't want to cough up the dough.

costar un ojo de la cara

to cost an arm and a leg, lit. to cost an eye off the face

Un buen sombrero de mariachi cuesta un ojo de la cara.

A good mariachi hat costs an arm and a leg.

costar un huevo y la mitad del otro

to cost a fortune, lit. to cost a ball (egg) and half the other

**Este traje de charro me costó un huevo y la mitad
    del otro.**

This charro suit cost me a fortune.

cuentachiles, m (Mexico)

penny-pincher, lit. chile-counter

**Mi jefe es un cuentachiles, siempre me revista los
    gastos.**

My boss is a penny-pincher, always looking over my expenses.

borrega, f (Mexico)

wallet, lit. ewe

**Yo creo que este tío es camello, pues siempre trae
    llena la borrega.**

*I think this guy's a drug dealer because his wallet is always
    full.*

lit. I think this guy is a camel because his ewe is always full.

cagar dinero lana

to have lot of cash, lit. to shit money

**Por el coche que traen, se ve que los nuevos vecinos
    cagan lana.**

*You can see by their fancy car that the new neighbors have a
    lot of cash.*

despelucar
to be left without a dime, lit. to de-wig someone
No vayas al hipódromo; te van a despelucar.
Don't go to the races; you will be left without a dime.

de gorra
without paying, lit. of hat
Nadie invitó a los chiquillos; se metieron de gorra.
Nobody invited the schoolkids; they snuck in without paying.

domingo, m
allowance / pocket money, lit. Sunday
Si se entera mi tío que reprobé inglés, ya no me va a dar mi domingo.
If my uncle finds out I failed English, he will not give me my weekly allowance.

entre pitos y flautas
willy-nilly, lit. among whistles and flutes
Entre pitos y flautas, gastamos 250 pesos en el mall.
We spent $250 at the mall willy-nilly.

encajoso, m
bum, lit. creep
Aarón es un encajoso; nunca ofrece pagar nada.
Aarón is a bum; he never offers to pay for anything.

en pelotas, en bolas
to be broke, lit. in the balls
Después de cinco días en Las Vegas, me quedé en pelotas.
After five days in Las Vegas, I was completely broke.

estar botado

to be inexpensive, lit. to be thrown out

¿Sólo cuesta $100? ¡Este vestido está botado!

It only cost $100? That dress is a steal!

estar en la calle

to end up on the street, lit. to be in the street

**Si el seguro no nos cubre el accidente del coche, nos
quedamos en la calle.**

*If the insurance doesn't cover the car accident, we'll end up
on the street.*

estar forrado

to have a lot of money, lit. to be lined

Mi amigo Colin está forrado.

My friend Colin has a lot of money.

ganar el oro y el moro

to make a very good living, lit. to earn the gold and the Moor

El dueño de la fábrica donde trabajo gana el oro y el moro.

The owner of the factory where I work makes a very good living.

hacer su agosto

to make a killing, lit. to make one's August

**Con este calor que hace, el vendedor de helados va a
hacer su agosto.**

With this heat, the ice-cream vendor is going to make a killing.

hacer agua

to flounder, lit. to leak water

El negocio de joyería de mi papá ya empezó a hacer agua.

My dad's jewelry business has started to flounder.

lit. My dad's jewelry business has begun to leak water.

hijo de papá, m

rich kid, lit. son of dad

A ese hijo de papá le han comprado un coche nuevo y no trabaja para nada.

That rich kid just got a new car and he doesn't work at all.

lana, f (Mexico)

dough, money, lit. wool

El abogado y su mujer se fueron del país con toda la lana de sus clientes.

The lawyer and his wife left the country with all their clients' money.

limosnero y con garrote, m

beggars can't be choosers, lit. beggar with a stick

El mendigo me pidió dinero, pero no quiere monedas. ¡Es un limosnero con garrote!

The bum asked for money but wouldn't take coins. Beggars can't be choosers!

mano rota, f

spendthrift, lit. broken hand

Mi hermana nunca ahorra un quinto; es una mano rota.

My sister will never save a penny; she's such a spendthrift.

morena, f (Mexico)

safe, lit. brunette

Necesitamos la combinación para abrir la morena.

We need the combination to open the safe.

muerto/muerta de hambre

stingy bastard, lit. dying of hunger

Mike no nos pagó el desayuno; es un muerto de hambre.

Mike didn't pay for our breakfast; what a stingy bastard.

negra, f

safe, lit. black one

Abrieron la negra en menos de cinco minutos.

The safe was picked in less than five minutes.

no tener lana (Mexico)

to have no money, lit. to have no wool

No puedo salir esta noche; no tengo lana.

I can't go out tonight; I have no money.

papiros, mpl

bills/money, lit. papyrus

Me encantó ese vestido de Gucci, pero costaba muchos papiros.

I loved that Gucci dress, but it was too expensive.

pagar el pato

to pay the piper, lit. to pay for the duck

Los amigos de Clara se salieron sin pagar, y a ella le tocó pagar el pato.

Clara's friends left without paying the bill and she had to pay the piper.

pagar los platos rotos

to pay the price, lit. to pay for the broken plates

¡Pobre Carlos! Siempre acaba pagando los platos rotos.

Poor Carlos! He always ends up paying the price.

pasta (Spain)
dough, lit. pasta
Los futbolistas de Europa se meten una pasta.
Soccer stars in Europe make dough.

no tener un mango (Argentina)
to not have a dime, lit. to not have a mango/handle
Desde la devaluación, nadie tiene un mango.
Ever since the devaluation, people don't have a dime.

oro molido
very valuable, lit. crushed gold
¡No tires tus chanclas! En la playa son oro molido.
Don't get rid of your flip-flops; they are very valuable at the beach.

oro negro, m
oil, lit. black gold
México exporta oro negro.
Mexico exports a lot of oil.

palos, mpl
money, lit. sticks
No puedo creer que pagué veinte palos por estos pantalones tan feos.
I cannot believe I paid twenty bucks for this pair of ugly pants.

panzona, f
wallet, lit. big belly
Mi mejor amigo traía la panzona bien llena y nos invitó una hora de mariachis.
My best friend had a full wallet; so he bought us one hour of mariachis.

pedir las perlas de la virgen

to ask for the queen's jewels, lit. to ask for the pearls of
the Virgin

**Susana quería darle el trabajo al chico bilingüe, pero
le pidió las perlas de la virgen.**

*Susana wanted to give the job to the bilingual kid, but he
asked for the queen's jewels.*

plata, f

money, lit. silver

**Me quiero comprar un Lamborghini pero cuesta
mucha plata.**

*I want to buy myself a Lamborghini but it costs a lot of
money.*

ponerse guapo

to pick up the tab, lit. to make oneself good-looking

**Para celebrar el cumpleaños número treinta de
Rodrigo, su esposa se puso guapa y nos invitó
a todos a un restaurante elegante.**

*To celebrate his thirtieth birthday, Rodrigo's wife picked up
the tab and invited us all to a fancy restaurant.*

pegarle al gordo

to hit the jackpot, lit. to hit the fat guy

Un número más y le pegamos al gordo.

One number more and we'll hit the jackpot.

sacarse la polla (Latin America)

to hit the jackpot, lit. to take out the hen

¡Si no fuera por un número, la mujer del policía se hubiera sacado la polla!

If it wasn't for one number, the cop's wife would have hit the jackpot!

suelto, m

change, lit. loose

Hay que cambiar el billete de $100. No traigo suelto.

We need to change a $100 bill. We have no change.

CHAPTER ELEVEN

De pinta:
Work and School

When it comes to working hard, no other group in the United States has a better reputation than Mexicans. While those Mexican Americans with several generations of U.S. citizenship have been nearly fully integrated into all levels of the workforce, many recent arrivals remain in manual labor jobs. In California, the largest agricultural producer in the United States, not many farms could survive without the help of Mexican or Central American immigrants. Dedicated, hard-working and, sadly, low-paid, these workers do the jobsmany others are too lazy to do. And what's more, they do it with a smile and a thank-you.

acordeón, m (Mexico)
cheat sheet, lit. accordion
No estudié nada, pero como llevaba un acordeón me saqué diez en el examen.
I didn't study a bit, but since I used a cheat sheet I got an A on the test.

a la brava
bald-faced, without care or concern, lit. fiercely
Mi prima me quitó el novio a la brava.
My cousin snatched my boyfriend away just like that.

a trancas y barrancas (Spain)
with great difficulty, lit. at cudgel and precipices
Terminé el examen a trancas y barrancas.
I finished the exam with great difficulty.

al ahí se va
half-assed job, lit. there it goes
Ese plomero me cae mal; siempre hace las cosas al ahí se va.
I don't like that plumber; he always does a half-assed job.

aviador, m (Mexico)
someone who is on the payroll but doesn't actually work, lit. air pilot
Esta oficina está llena de aviadores.
That office is full of people who are on the payroll but don't actually work.

barco, m (Mexico)
easy, lit. ship
Nuestra maestra siempre nos deja hacer trampa en el examen; es muy barco.
Our teacher always lets us cheat during tests; she's easy.

chupatintas, m

office worker/bureaucrat, lit. ink-licker

Mi vecino dice que es un alto ejecutivo, pero no es más que un chupatintas.

My neighbor says he is a senior executive, but he's nothing but an office worker.

de entrada por salida

day worker/live-out worker, lit. of entry and exit

María va a empezar a trabajar conmigo el lunes, pero de entrada por salida.

Maria will start working for me on Monday, but as a live-out maid.

de panzazo

barely, lit. of the stomach

Con el seis que nos sacamos en matemáticas, mi hermano y yo pasamos la secundaria de panzazo.

With the Cs we got in math, my brother and I barely passed secondary school.

devanarse los sesos

to think really hard, lit. to wind one's brains

Por más que me devané los sesos, no pude resolver el problema de mate.

No matter how hard I thought about it, I couldn't solve the math problem.

estar cañón

to be really hard, lit. to be cannon

Este proyecto de química está cañón. No sé si pueda hacerlo.

This chemistry project is really hard. I´m not sure I will be able to do it.

estar en chino
to be very difficult, lit. to be in Chinese
La receta del pavo está en chino.
The recipe for this turkey is very difficult.

estar pelón
to be extremely difficult, lit. to be bald
¡Este crucigrama está pelón!
This crossword puzzle is extremely difficult!

estira y afloja
to negotiate, lit. stretch and loose
**Todavía no llegamos a nada; seguimos en el estira y
    afloja.**
*We have not yet reached an agreement; we're still
    negotiating.*

¡está grueso!
hard/heavy, lit. it's thick
**Suerte con el examen de la Barra; yo lo hice el año
    pasado y ¡está grueso!**
*Good luck with the Bar exam; I took it last year and it's really
    hard!*

capear clase (Colombia)
to skip class, lit. to avoid class
**Los muchachos se capearon clase y pasaron todo el día
    en la playa.**
The kids skipped class and spent all day in the beach.

Hispanic students aren't so different from other children. They all have to go to school and do their homework, though some are not keen to do so. The answer? Skipping school or playing hookie—*hacer la rata*, "making the rat," is much more interesting than math. While we're talking animals (some kids could pass as one), students may *volarse la clase*, "fly from class," or manage to sneak away unnoticed in Chile by *hacer la cimarra*, "making the small insect." Some Mexican children prefer *irse de pinta*, "to go as paint" rather than to follow their lessons. For those aspiring artists, *pintar venado*, "painting deer," is a good compromise. Don't get this one? Think about *les grottes de Lascaux* in France; Mexican children might daydream about painting in caves as primitive humans did in the caves at Lascaux. Another expression for playing hookie is connected with fruit. When a student is bored, there's nothing better than *tirarse la pera*, "throwing oneself the pear." Just don't throw it at the teacher!

echar la güeva
to do nothing, lit. to throw a fish egg
Esos albañiles nunca hacen nada productivo; siempre están echando la güeva, tomando café.
Those construction workers never do anything productive; they are always there doing nothing but drinking coffee.

flojo, floja

lazy, lit. loose

Mi hermano es un flojo; no ha salido todo el día.

My brother is very lazy; he hasn't left the house all day.

hueso, m (Mexico)

government job, lit. bone

Tan pronto nombren alcalde a mi tío, seguro me da un hueso.

As soon as my uncle is made mayor, he will give me a government job.

más fácil que la tabla del uno

easy, lit. easier than multiplying one times one

La cajera de la zapatería se va con todos; es más fácil que la tabla del uno.

The cashier from the shoe store goes out with anyone; she's easy.

más flojo que el algodon de borla

very lazy, lit. looser than cotton balls

¿Tu hijo ni siquiera tiende su cama?; es más flojo que el algodón de borla.

Your son doesn't even make his bed? How lazy of him.

no dar palo al agua

to fail to do anything right, lit. to not beat the water with a stick

Seguro Mateo no pasa el curso; pues no da palo al agua.

Mateo will surely fail the course; he can't do anything right.

no dar pie con bola

to not do anything right/to not get it, lit. to not give foot with ball

Le explicamos todo tres veces a Kati, pero no da pie con bola.

We explained things three times to Kati, but she still doesn't get it!

partirse la madre

to work one's ass off, lit. to break one's mother

Se partió la madre trabajando para sus hijos y ni se lo agradecen.

She worked her ass off for her children, and they don't even thank her.

pegárseles las cobijas

to oversleep, lit. to have the sheets stuck to your body

Gloria dijo que llegó tarde por el tráfico, pero yo creo que se le pegaron las cobijas.

Gloria said she was late because of the traffic, but I think she just overslept.

quemarse las pestañas

to burn the candle at both ends, lit. to burn one's eyelashes

Más vale que me ponga diez la maestra; anoche me quemé las pestañas estudiando.

The teacher had better give me an A; I burned the candle at both ends for the exam.

sacar el jugo a algo

to make the most of something, lit. to take the juice out of something

Hay que llegar temprano para sacarle jugo al curso.

Let's show up early to make the most out of the course.

ser de armas tomar
to be a piece of work, lit. to be of taking weapons
Cuidado con Karen, es de armas tomar.
Beware of Karen. She's a real piece of work.

estar hasta los huevos
to be tired, lit. to be up to the balls (eggs)
Estoy hasta los huevos de mi patrón.
I've had it with my boss!
lit. I'm up to the eggs / up to the balls with my boss!

ser huevón
to be lazy, lit. to be a big egg
¡Eres un huevón!
You're such a lazy one.

tener hueva
to be tired, lit. to have female egg
No quiero ir a la escuela; tengo mucha hueva.
I don't want to go to school, I'm very tired.

tumbaburros, m
dictionary, lit. donkey-dumper
**Para que aprendas a deletrear, Juan te va a regalar
un tumbaburros.**
Juan will give you a dictionary so you can learn to spell.

CHAPTER TWELVE

Policías y ladrones:
The Wrong Side of the Law

The *Estados Unidos's* infamous war on drugs has been anything but bad for Latin American *coca* growers. As much of the cocaine produced here goes to directly to satisfy the United States's big appetite for the powerful white powder, business has remained steady despite their best efforts. Some high-producing *país,* namely Colombia, may have a terrible *reputación,* but in fact *coca* has a long history in this part of the world.

The plant is native to the Andes and is commonly used in Peru, Colombia, Ecuador, Venezuela, and Bolivia. Mind you, the *coca* leaf is not cocaine; it contains several different alkaloids, only one of which is cocaine. Cocaine as we know it is then the extracted cocaine alkaloid of this leaf. Sacred for its nutritional and medicinal properties, the *coca* leaf can be found in soaps, shampoos and other beauty products. It is also consumed regularly as an herbal tea, and has a stimulating effect similar to that of strong coffee. Full of protein and vitamins, it is often it is chewed by native peoples to maintain endurance during tiring walks in the high-altitude mountains.

archivar

to put into jail, lit. to file

Nos archivaron a todos por estar en la escena del delito cuando llegó la poli.

We were all sent to jail for being at the crime scene when the cops arrived.

azul, m (Mexico)

cop, lit. blue

Tan pronto los llamamos, llegaron los azules.

The cops showed up as soon as we called them.

bajar

to steal / to take away, lit. to lower down

Dos pandilleros me bajaron la cartera en el metro.

Two gangbangers stole my wallet in the subway.

bailar

to steal/swindle, lit. to dance

Andrés, mi compañero de clase, me bailó los apuntes otra vez.

My fellow student Andrés stole my notes again.

balconear a alguien

to rat on/out someone, lit. to balcony someone

Me escondí debajo de la cama para que no me vieran los papás de mi novia, pero el hermanito me balconeó.

I hid under the bed so that my girlfriend's parents wouldn't see me, but her little brother ratted on me.

caballo, m (Spain)

smack, heroin, lit. horse

El alcalde se fue preso porque la policía lo pilló con caballo en el carro.

The mayor went to jail because the police found smack in his car.

camello, m

drug dealer, lit. camel

Todos saben que tu primo es camello, pero como tiene amigos en la policía no le pasa nada.

Everybody knows your cousin is a drug dealer, but since he has friends in the police department, nothing will ever happen to him.

cangrejo, m (Spain)

cop, lit. crab

Nos salimos corriendo antes de que llegaran los cangrejos.

We got the hell out before the cops showed up.

casa grande, f

jail, lit. big house

Son quince años en la casa grande por robar coches.

It's fifteen years in the big house for stealing cars.

cajón, m (Spain)

jail, lit. drawer

Mandaron a Marcos al cajón aunque era inocente.

Marcos was sent to jail even though he was innocent.

(en) cana
(in) jail, lit. grey hair
Pedro estuvo en cana un mes por robarle dinero a su patrón.
Pedro spent a month in jail for stealing money from his boss.

canuto, m (Spain)
joint, lit. tube/blowpipe
Antes de entrar al concierto nos fumamos un canuto.
We had a joint before the concert.

cantar
to rat out, lit. to sing
Después de un interrogatorio de cuarenta y ocho horas, el mafioso cantó como canario.
After he was grilled for forty-eight hours, the Mafioso sang like a canary.

churro, m (Mexico)
joint, lit. churro
El profesor cachó a sus estudiantes fumándose un churro.
The teacher caught his students smoking a joint.

clavarse algo
to steal, lit. to nail something in
Cada vez que vamos al restaurant chino, nos clavamos los ceniceros.
Every time we go to the Chinese restaurant, we steal the ashtrays.

charola, f
police badge, lit. tray
El que nos detuvo andaba vestido de civil, pero luego sacó la charola.
The cop who stopped us was in plainclothes, but he took out his badge immediately.

chayote, m
bribe given to journalists, lit. chayote (a vegetable)
Esa periodista siempre escribe bien del presidente; vive del puro chayote.
That journalist is always writing nice things about the president; she lives on pure bribes.

chueco, chueca
fake, lit. twisted
A leguas se nota que ese Rolex es chueco.
You can see from a mile away that Rolex is fake.

diablito, m
device used to steal electricity, lit. little devil
Con razón los vecinos no pagaban casi nada de electricidad; tenían instalado un diablito.
No wonder our neighbors pay almost nothing for electricity; they've installed a device to steal it!

doña blanca
cocaine, lit. Mrs. White
Traía de todo en la maleta, desde mota hasta doña blanca.
He had everything in that suitcase, from weed to cocaine.

echar aguas

to look out, lit. to throw water

Échame aguas mientras me meto por la ventana.

Look out while I sneak through the window.

echar el guante

to catch somebody, lit. to throw the glove

EL FBI le echó el guante a los secuestradores cuando la chica todavía estaba viva.

The FBI caught the kidnappers while the abducted girl was still alive.

escabechar (Mexico)

to kill, lit. to pickle

Los narcos de Tijuana se escabecharon a diez policías durante la redada.

The drug dealers from Tijuana killed ten cops in the raid.

escandalosa, f

siren, lit. loud one

Los intrusos se fueron huyendo tan pronto oyeron la escandalosa.

The trespassers got the hell out as soon as they heard the siren.

ir al bote

to go to jail, lit. to go to the boat

Si sigues vendiendo drogas a los chicos, vas a acabar en el bote.

If you continue to sell drugs to kids, you'll end up in jail.

Jail seems to be a very popular subject of conversation for many Spanish-speaking people; at least one would think so based on the dozens of slang words to describe it: people get into trouble and end up in *la casa grande*, "the big house," *el bote*, "the boat," *el cajón*, "the drawer," *cana*, "gray hair," or *la alcancía*, "the piggy bank"; in *el tambo, la cafúa, la chirona, la gayola, la jaula* (all meaning "cage"); in *la peni*, "penitentiary"; in *el talego* or *la perrera* (both meaning "the dog house"); in *la madrastra*, "the stepmother," or *multifamiliar*, "housing project."

escurrir el bulto

to dodge the question, lit. to drain the package

Simon no quiere hablar del problema; siempre escurre el bulto.

Simon doesn't want to talk about his problem; he always dodges the question.

llevar al baile

to cheat/swindle, lit. to take to the ball/dance

Ese contador nos llevó al baile con la última declaración de impuestos.

That accountant swindled us with his latest tax schemes.

maletas, f, m

bad, awful, lit. suitcases

Los íbamos a contratar como empleados domésticos, pero son muy maletas.

We were going to hire them as housecleaners, but they were very awful.

maría, f (Spain)

mary jane, pot, lit. Maria

Tira la maría antes de subirte al avión.

Get rid of the mary jane before you board the plane.

meterse en camisa de once varas

to get into a tricky situation, lit. to be put in a shirt of eleven
sticks

**Cuando acepté escribir este libro, no imaginé que me
metiera en camisa de once varas.**

*When I agreed to write this book, I didn't know I would get
into this tricky situation!*

mota, f (Mexico)

marijuana, lit. speck of dust

**En todo el mundo, a los adolescentes y a los hippies les
encanta la mota.**

All over the world, teenagers and hippies like to smoke weed.

meter la uña

to steal, lit. to stick in the fingernail

El jefe despidió a su asistente por meter la uña.

The boss fired his assistant for stealing.

movida, f

fishy situation, lit. moved

**No sé en qué anda metido mi novio, pero no me gustan
sus movidas.**

*I'm not sure what my boyfriend is up to, but I don't like the
fishy situations he gets into.*

orégano, m
weed, lit. oregano
Mi mamá nos cachó con un cigarro de orégano.
My mom caught us with a joint.

palancas, fpl
connections, lit. handles
Mi padrino tiene muchas palancas en el gobierno.
My godfather has a lot of connections in the government.

pagar los platos rotos
to pay for a crime one didn't commit, lit. to pay for the broken
    plates
**Como siempre, tú te quedas tan tranquilo y es a mi a
    quien le toca pagar los platos rotos.**
*As always, you're so calm and it's me who ends up paying for
    a crime I didn't commit.*

paracaidista, f, m
squatters, illegal tenant, lit. parachuter
**Los paracaidistas llevaban años viviendo en esa casa
    abandonada sin pagar renta.**
*The squatters have been living in that abandoned house for
    years without paying rent.*

pasar la báscula
to be searched, lit. to pass the scale
**Nos dejaron entrar en la discoteca pero después de
    pasarnos báscula.**
We were let into the disco after first being searched.

pegar el muerto

to walk out without paying, lit. to stick the dead one

Ahora que los meseros no están mirando, vamos a pegarnos el muerto.

Now that the waiters are not watching, let's leave without paying.

meterse un pericazo

to snort cocaine, lit. to put oneself a big parrot

Papi anda todo alborotado; parece que se metió un pericazo.

Daddy's all wired up; looks like he snorted some cocaine.

poner un cuatro

to set someone up, lit. to put a four

Le pusieron un cuatro al mensajero y confesó que se había robado los cheques.

They set the delivery boy up and he confessed to stealing the checks.

rata, f

crook, lit. rat

El dueño de la bodega es bien rata; cobra 100 pesos por un six de cervezas.

The owner of the grocery store is a crook; he charges 100 pesos for a six pack of beer.

sacar a alguien del hoyo

to get someone out of a mess, lit. to take someone out of the hole

Qué bueno que llamaste a mi abogado; estoy seguro de que él me va a sacar del hoyo.

I'm glad you called my lawyer; I'm sure he'll get me out of this mess.

salir volando

to rush off, lit. to leave flying

Cuando me vieron venir hacia ellos con un bat de béisbol, los muchachos salieron volando.

When the guys saw me coming toward them with a baseball bat, they rushed off.

contar a alguien santo y seña de algo

to give someone the dirt on something, lit. to tell someone saint and signal

Tan pronto regresó, Juanita nos contó santo y seña de su luna de miel.

As soon as she came back Juanita gave us all the dirt on her honeymoon.

tamarindo, m (Mexico)

traffic cop, lit. tamarind

No te vayas a dar la vuelta aquí; hay mucho tamarindo.

Don't make an illegal turn here; there are a lot of traffic cops around.

tartamuda, f

machine gun, lit. stutterer

Los escoltas del político traían todos una tartamuda.

The politician's bodyguards were all carrying machine guns.

transas

cheat/swindler, lit. to trade

Los guardias del edificio son muy transas; siempre se roban el correo.

The guards at my office building are such cheats; they steal the mail.

tronárselas

to smoke pot, lit. to thunder oneself

En la prepa, todos se las tronaban en el baño.

In high school, everybody smokes pot in the bathroom.

uñilarga

thief, lit. long nails

Cuidado con Juanito; es muy uñilarga.

Beware of Juanito; he's a real thief.

volar

to steal / take away, lit. to fly

Los niños fueron al supermercado y se volaron un montón de dulces.

The kids went to the supermarket and stole a lot of candy.

CHAPTER THIRTEEN

Estirar la pata:
Of Health and Death

El Día de los Muertos, Day of the Dead, is much more than a Mexican version of Halloween. Held on November 1 (Day of the Little Dead—children) and November 2 (Day of the Adult Dead), the sacred days actually date back to pre-Catholic times. The conquering Spanish were clever to align these days with their own Catholic All Saints' Day, allowing for the easy integration of the festival into the New World.

Traditionally, families honor the dead, *los muertos,* on these days by visiting the gravesites of their ancestors and offering *comida,* drink, and decorations. It is thought that *los muertos* can communicate with those on *la tierra* during this time if the living do certain things, like leave an orange marigold flower on the graves of the dead. A visit to a *cementerio* on these nights (be sure to bring *dinero* for the entry fee . . .) will not be the somber, solemn affair you might expect. *Mariachis* abound and will sing a song for the deceased for a small fee, and drinking and dancing have made *Día de los Muertos* one of the biggest *fiestas* of the year.

aliviarse

to give birth, lit. to be cured (Mexico)

La mucama se alivió de gemelos.

The maid gave birth to twins.

botársele la canica

to lose one's marbles, lit. to have a marble loose

Sierra está hablando puras tonterías. Ya se le botó la canica.

Sierra is talking a lot of nonsense. I think she's lost her marbles.

cargar con el muertito

to be the fall guy, lit. to carry the dead body

Ellos tuvieron la culpa y ahora a mí me toca cargar con el muertito.

It was their fault, but yet they made me the fall guy.

colgar los tenis

to kick the bucket, lit. to hang up the sneakers

El viejo por fin colgó los tenis.

The old man kicked the bucket.

lit. At last, the old man hung up the sneakers.

comer el tarro

to brainwash, lit. to eat the jar

Claro que ya no quiere ir con nosotros; a Alexandra le comieron el tarro.

Of course she doesn't want to come with us; Alexandra has been brainwashed.

comerse la torta antes del recreo

to get pregnant out of wedlock, lit. to eat the sandwich before lunchtime

La hija de la muchacha tiene catorce años, y ya se comió la torta antes del recreo.

The maid's fourteen-year-old daughter is already pregnant out of wedlock.

cruzársele los cables [a alguien]

to be confused, lit. to have the cables crossed

A Luis se le cruzaron los cables, pensó que hoy era domingo y por eso no llegó al desayuno de negocios.

Luis got confused; he thought today was Sunday and didn't show up for his important breakfast meeting.

chupar faros

to bite the dust, lit. to suck the headlights

El perro ése al que atropellaron ya chupó faros.

That dog that was run over bit the dust.

edad de la punzada

adolescent, lit. the age of the sharp pain

Carlita está insoportable; ¡claro! Está en la edad de la punzada.

Carlita's unbearable. Of course, she's a teenager!

entregar el equipo

to die, lit. to hand over the equipment

La viejita ya está muy mal; seguro pronto entrega el equipo.

The old lady is in bad shape; I am sure she'll die soon.

enfermarse (Mexico)

to have one's period, lit. to be sick

Mis dos hermanas se enfermaron al mismo tiempo.

My two sisters had their period at the same time.

estar en las últimas

to be dying, lit. to be in the last ones

Los enfermos de ese piso están en las últimas.

The patients on this floor are all dying.

estar mal de la azotea

to be out of one's mind, lit. to be sick in the roof

¿Quieres volver a ver esa película? ¡Estás mal de la azotea!

You want to see that movie again? You are out of your mind!

estar zafado

to be nuts, lit. to be loosened up

No sé ni qué me dices; estás zafado.

I have no idea what you're saying; you're nuts.

estirar la pata

to kick the bucket, lit. to straighten the leg

Dile a tu papá que firme su testamento antes que estire la pata.

Tell your father to sign his will before he kicks the bucket.

faltarle un fusible a alguien

to be ditzy, lit. to be missing a fuse

A mi mamá siempre se le olvidan las cosas; yo creo que le falta un fusible.

My mom is always forgetting things; I think she's missing a fuse.

faltarle un tornillo a alguien

to have screw loose, lit. to be missing a screw

No hagas caso a lo que dice el presidente; ¡le falta un tornillo!

Don't listen what the president has to say; he's got a screw loose!

flaca, f

death, lit. skinny one

¡Si siguen chupando así, Toby, se los va a llevar la flaca!

If you keep drinking like that, Toby, you'll die!

hacerla de tos

to make a fuss, lit. to make it of cough

¡Sólo reprobé tres materias, mamá! No la hagas de tos.

I only flunked three classes, Mom! Don't make a fuss about it.

huesuda, f

death, lit. bony one

El abuelo de mi novio ya está muy viejito; yo creo que la huesuda ya se lo va a llevar.

My boyfriend's grandpa is very old; I think he will die soon.

mujer en estado, f

pregnant woman, lit. woman in state

Había varios niños y una mujer en estado en el autobús.

There were several children and a pregnant woman on the bus.

más loco (a) que una cabra

crazier than a loon, lit. crazier than a goat

¡Ese muchacho es más loco que una cabra!

This kid is crazier than a loon.

matasanos, m

doctor, lit. healthy people-killer

Mi abuelo se puso tan mal después de haberme gritado, que tuvo que ir a ver al matasanos.

My grandpa felt so bad after yelling at me that he ended up going to the doctor.

mear fuera del tarro

to be off base, lit. to pee outside the jar

Yo no te eché de cabeza con tus papás; te estás meando fuera del tarro.

I didn't rat you out to your parents; you are way off base!

no poder ni con su alma

to be tired / exhausted, lit. not even with one's soul

Quieren que subamos hasta la cima del cerro, pero yo ya no puedo ni con mi alma.

They want us to go all the way to the top, but I'm exhausted.

parir chayotes

something of great difficulty, lit. to give birth to chayotes (a vegetable)

Mi jefe me puso a parir chayotes con la traducción de este texto legal.

My boss gave me a very difficult assignment in translating this legal text.

parar la chala (Chile)

to die, lit. to straighten the sandal

El abuelito de Carmen está tan viejito, que está a punto de estirar la chala.

Carmen's grandfather is so old that he's about to die.

patadas de ahogado
useless effort, lit. drowning man's kicks
Sabe que no lo va a conseguir; sus intentos son puras patadas de ahogado.
He knows he will not achieve that; his efforts are useless.
lit. He knows he won't achieve that, his intentions are pure drowning man's kicks.

patinarle el coco (a alguien)
to be losing one's mind, lit. to have one's coconut slipping
A Marisa le patina el coco.
Marisa seems to be losing her mind.

patinarle el embrague (a alguien)
to be crazy, lit. to have one's clutch slipping
Ayer me dijiste lo contrario; a mí se me hace que te patina el embrague.
You told me the exact opposite yesterday; I think you are crazy.

pelona, f
death, lit. bold one
Iba manejando tan rápido que vi de cerca a la pelona.
He was driving so fast that I saw death right before my eyes.

petatearse
to die, lit. to hit the petate (a typical Mexican rug)
Este señor ya se petateó.
This man has kicked the bucket.

ser la mar de tonto

to be a fool, lit. to be the sea of foolishness

El hermano de mi novia nunca entiende nada; es la mar de tonto.

My girlfriend's brother never understands anything; he's a fool.

CHAPTER FOURTEEN

De reventón:
Life is a Cabaret ... or Discotheque ... or House Party

For Hispanics, going out late is not only for young, swinging singles. Take a stroll in Madrid on a weekend, and you'll see whole families enjoying the warm summer nights until the wee hours of the morning. While the sight of a three-year-old *niño* in a park at midnight would raise real concern in the United States, in Spain it wouldn't be given a second thought. Whether eating ice cream cones or listening to street musicians playing accordion, everyone under the sun can be found out and about late into the night.

aduana, f (Mexico)
brothel, lit. customs house

Después del bar, los marineros se fueron a la aduana y lo pasaron muy bien.

After the bar, the sailors went to the brothel and had a really good time.

aguafiestas

killjoy, lit water party

Mejor no invites a tu hermano Peter; no le gusta tomar ni bailar y es un aguafiestas.

Better not invite your brother Peter; he doesn't drink or dance and is a real bore.

aburrirse como una ostra

to be bored to tears, lit. to be bored as an oyster

Cadavez que visito a mis tíos en el campo me aburro como una ostra.

Every time I visit my family in the countryside I'm bored to tears.

a las (mil) quinientas

the wee hours, lit. at the (one thousand) five hundreds

Cada vez que las niñas salen con Ned de fiesta, regresan a las mil quinientas.

Every time the girls go out with Ned, they come back in the wee hours.

a morir

until the end, lit. to die

La fiesta estuvo buenísima; nos quedamos bailando a morir.

The party was great; we were dancing until the end.

bailando la manzanilla

to move around, lit. to dance the chamomile

No he podido localizar a mi papá; siempre anda bailando la manzanilla.

I haven't been able to find my father; he's always moving around.

As in many other languages, there are plenty of words for prostitute in Spanish, beginning with perhaps the most common: *puta*. As there are even more customers than prostitutes, the words used to name those working girls come from many different genres.

Some artists will find inspiration in the arms of a *ninfa*, "nymph," or feel like a king surrounded by his *cortesanas*, "courtesans." When looking for adventure, the *aventurera*, "adventurous one," will be a good companion. A basic observation will lead you to call her *callejera*, "streetwalker," *cantonera*, "idler," or *mujer de la calle*, "street woman." Other aspects of the world's oldest job inspired the *calientacamas*, "bed-heater," and *horizontal*, "horizontal," for obvious reasons.

Nasty people may call a prostitute a *mujer pública*, "public woman," *regalada*, "given away," *cualquiera*, "anybody," *mantenida*, "maintained," *mujerzuela*, "little woman," *mujer de la vida*, "life's woman," *mundana*, "mundane one," or *buscona*, "seeker".

The slang term *germana*, "German," is certainly connected with the usual cliché about Germans and sex (if you've ever had the pleasure to see German porn, known as the raunchiest stuff out there, you know exactly what we mean). It's no wonder that in conservative societies some slang words reduce prostitutes to *pelleja*, "female flesh" —not even a person, just meat. The need to take any traces of humanity away from prostitutes leaves them considered as animals: *zorra*, "female fox," *changa*, "female monkey," or *perra*, "female dog."

bataclán

loud party, lit. bataclan (from the French *bataclan*, "junk")

El bataclán de los vecinos nos tuvo despiertos toda la noche.

The neighbor's loud party kept us up all night.

boliche, m

bar/club, lit. bowling alley

No pudimos entrar al boliche porque estaba lleno.

We couldn't get into the club because it was packed.

casa de citas

brothel, lit. house of appointments

La bodega no es más que una tapadera de la casa de citas de la Señora Chona.

The bodega is only a front to hide the brothel of Mrs. Chona.

ciento y la madre

everybody and his brother, lit. one hundred and the mother

No pudimos entrar a ese café porque éramos ciento y la madre.

We couldn't get into the café because we were a lot of people.

colado, m

party crasher, lit. strained

En mi boda había 100 invitados y como 20 colados.

At my wedding there were about 100 guests and 20 party crashers.

cotorrear

to chat/have fun, lit. to (talk like) a parrot

Nos quedamos cotorreando hasta las tres de la mañana.

We were chatting until three in the morning.

darle al cacle (Mexico)
to dance, lit. to give it to the shoe (from the Náhuatl *cactli*
    meaning "shoe")
Cansado o no, el juerguista no se cansó de darle al cacle.
Tired or not tired, the raver didn't stop dancing all night.

hotel de mala muerte, m
hooker's hotel, lit. hotel of bad death
Terminamos la noche en un hotel de mala muerte.
We ended up in a hooker's hotel.

echar relajo
to have fun, lit. to throw relaxation
Vámonos a echar relajo.
Let's go have fun.

en patota
out in a big group, lit. in a big foot
**Hay que ir a la playa esta semana pero en patota es
    más divertido.**
Let's go to the beach this week in a big group, it's more fun.

fumar como chacuacos
to smoke like a chimney, lit. to smoke like a Mexican chimney
**Busquemos la sección de fumar porque mis amigos
    fuman como chachuacos.**
*Let's look for the smoking section because my friends smoke
    like a chimney.*

hacer la sopa
to shuffle cards, lit. to make the soup
Al que pierda esta partida le toca hacer la sopa.
He who loses this game will shuffle next time.

salir de marcha (Spain)

to go out to party, lit. to go out to march

Esta noche nos toca salir de marcha.

Tonight, we'll go out to party.

madama/madrina/madre superiora/madrota

madam, lit. madam/godmother/mother superior/stepmother

**Heidi Fleiss es de las madamas más famosas del
   mundo.**

Heidi Fleiss is one of the most famous madams in the world.

mover el bote

to dance, lit. to move the boat

**Mi prima no es buena en la escuela, pero le encanta
   mover el bote.**

My cousin is not very good at school, but she loves to dance.

menear el callo

to dance, lit. to shake the callus

**Mi tía dijo que se sentía mal, pero meneó el callo toda
   la noche.**

My aunt said she felt bad, but she didn't stop dancing all night.

Pachuca

to have nil in card play, lit. Pachuca (a Mexican town)

Me ganas con un par de dos; yo tengo Pachuca.

You win with your pair of twos. I've got nothing.

padrote, m

pimp, lit. big father

**Susana es un encanto de chica, pero su padrote es
   peligrosísimo.**

Susana is a great girl, but her pimp is super dangerous.

pasarlo chancho (Chile)

to have a good time, lit. to pass it pig

Lo pasamos chancho en la fiesta de Maria.

We had a great time at Maria's party.

palomazo, m

jam session, lit. big dove

**¡La fiesta estuvo buenísima! La banda de Paco se echó
    un palomazo.**

The party was great! Paco's band had a jam session.

recalentado, m

leftovers, lit. re-heating

**No podemos ir a la cena el sábado, pero llegamos el
    domingo al recalentado.**

*We can't make it to the dinner on Saturday, but will be there
    Sunday instead.*

reventón, m (Mexico)

party, lit. big explosion

¡Vámonos de reventón!

Let's go out and party!

zona rosa, f

red light district, lit. pink zone

¿En dónde está la zona rosa?

Where's the red light district?

CHAPTER FIFTEEN

Mezclando el tocino con la velocidad:
Mixed Bag

As the title of this chapter suggests, *Talk Dirty: Spanish* mixes bacon with speed, or *confundir el culo con las Témporas*, "confuses the ass with the Ember days." More accurately, the following handy slang expressions cannot be classified into other specific chapters. Consider it a mixed bag, like a wise *tonto* once said, a box of chocolates—you never know what you're gonna get.

a Chuchita la bolsearon
to come up with a lame excuse for something, lit. Chuchita was robbed/assaulted
Me prometiste llevarme al cine; ¡no me salgas ahora con que a Chuchita la bolsearon!
You promised to take me to the movies. Don't come up now with some lame excuse not to!

abrir cancha
to make room, lit. to open court (field)
¡Abran cancha que aquí viene la comida!
Make some room; here comes the food!

a ojo de buen cubero

to guess, lit. with the eye of a good *cubero* (someone who fills
up buckets of water)

**A ojo de buen cubero, calculo que la pintura alcanza
para todo el cuarto.**

I guess we have enough paint to cover this room.

agarrar a alguien en curva

to catch someone off-guard, lit. to grab someone in a curve

**Mi novio me agarró en curva cuando me pidió matrimo-
nio sólo dos semanas después de que empezamos
a salir.**

*My boyfriend caught me off-guard when he asked me to marry
him after only two weeks of dating.*

agarrar de bajada (a alguien)

to make fun of somebody, lit. to grab someone downhill

**Los otros estudiantes agarraron a Jack de bajada
porque invitó a salir a la más fea.**

*The other students made fun of Jack because he asked the
ugliest girl out.*

al chile

(get) to the point, lit. to the chile

Si tienes que decirme algo, dímelo ahora, al chile.

If you have something to tell me go ahead—get to the point.

armarse la gorda

all hell broke loose, lit. to arm oneself the fat one

**Estábamos bailando muy tranquilos cuando de pronto
se armó la gorda en el club**

*We were dancing quietly when all of a sudden all hell broke
loose in the club.*

bailar con la más fea

to be up shit's creek, lit. to dance with the ugliest girl

Al profesor de literatura le pagan mal y le dan la peor clase; siempre le toca bailar con la más fea.

The literature professor is poorly paid and gets the worst class; he's always up shit's creek.

barajar algo más despacio

to explain something more slowly, lit. to shuffle the cards slowly

No entendí nada de la historia que me contaste; barajé mela más despacio.

I didn't understand the story you just told me; explain it again slowly, please.

caer el Chahuistle

to show up unexpectedly, lit. for the plague to fall

Estábamos a punto de cenar cuando nos cayó el cha-huistle mi suegra con toda su familia.

We were about to sit down for dinner when my mother-in-law showed up with all her family.

caer el veinte

to get it, lit. to have the twenty cent coin fall

Le tuve que explicar la misma cosa mil veces hasta que a Max le cayó el veinte.

We had to explain the same thing a thousand times until Max finally got it.

caerse de culo/caerse los chones

to fall on one's ass/to be astonished, lit. for the ass/under-wear to fall down

Cuando le dije lo que ganaba se cayó de culo

When I told him how much money I made he fell on his ass.

cerrar con broche de oro

to finish on a high note, lit. to close with a golden zipper

**El concierto de The Police cerró con broche de oro
cuando cantaron "Roxanne."**

*The Police concert ended on a high note when the band
played "Roxanne."*

como Dios manda

properly, lit. as God orders

**No quiero comer aquí en el coche; vamos a la mesa a
comer como Dios manda.**

*I don't want to eat here in the car; let's sit down on the table
and eat properly.*

con bombo y platillo

with fanfare, lit. with drums and plates

La pareja anunció su matrimonio con bombo y platillo.

The couple announced their marriage with much fanfare.

cuento chino

story, lit. Chinese tale

**No hice la tarea, pero le conté un cuento chino a la
maestra y me creyó todo.**

*I didn't do my homework, but I made up a story for the teacher
and she fell for it.*

culebrón

soap opera/telenovela, lit. big serpent

**Mi abuela y mi mamá no se pierden por nada su
culebrón.**

*My grandmother and mother wouldn't miss their soap opera
for the world.*

dar en la torre

to break/spoil something, lit. to give in the tower

El agua del mar le dio en la torre a mi reloj.

The sea water ruined my watch.

dar el avión

to agree with someone all the time just to avoid confrontation, lit. to give someone the airplane

Mi mamá me preguntó si se veía bonita y le dije que sí sólo para darle el avión.

My mom asked me if she looked good and I said yes just to avoid confrontation.

dar al traste

to spoil a plan, lit. to give a pan

La lluvia dio al traste con mis planes de ir al campo.

The rain spoiled my plans to go to the country.

darse de santos

to be thankful for something, lit. to give oneself of saints

Dáte de santos que nos dieron cacahuates en el avión; por estos días ya no dan nada.

Be thankful they gave us peanuts on the plane; these days you don't get anything.

dar en el clavo

to hit the nail on the head, lit. to hit the nail

El médico le dio en el clavo con su diagnóstico.

The doctor hit the nail on the head with his diagnosis.

dar una cachetada con guante blanco

to insult someone in a very stylish/elegant way, lit. to slap
   someone with a white glove

**Aunque la maestra me insultó, al otro día le llevé una
   manzana para darle una cachetada con guante blanco.**

*Although the teacher told me I was an idiot, I brought her an
   apple the next day just to insult her in an elegant manner.*

darse baños de pureza

to pretend to be really innocent, lit. to take baths of purity

**Nuestra vecina se ha metido con todo el vecindario, y
   aun así se da sus baños de pureza.**

*Our neighbor has slept with everybody yet she pretends to be
   very innocent.*

de miedo

great, lit. of fear

¡Mi novio se compró una motocicleta de miedo!

My boyfriend bought himself a great motorcycle!

de perdida

at least, lit. of lost

**No había qué comer en el bautizo; de perdida nos hubi-
   eran dado una cerveza.**

*There was no food at the baptism; at least they could have
   given us a beer.*

dorar la píldora

to sugar-coat, lit. to gild the pill

**El abogado no nos quería decir nada en concreto; se la
   pasó dorándonos la píldora.**

*The attorney didn't want to give us any specifics; he kept
   sugar-coating things.*

echar en saco roto

to throw away/waste, lit. to throw in a broken coat

Nunca eches los buenos consejos en saco roto.

Never throw away good advice.

echar la bolita (a alguien)

to put the blame on (somebody), lit. to throw the little ball
(to someone)

**Yo no tuve nada que ver con eso; a mí me echaron la
bolita.**

I had nothing to do with that, somebody put the blame on me.

estar en pañales

naïve, lit. to wear diapers

**En cuestiones de sexo, las chicas del colegio católico
están en pañales.**

When it comes to sex, Catholic schoolgirls are really naïve.

hacer changuitos

to cross one's fingers wishing good luck, lit. to make little
monkeys

**¡Haz changuitos para que nos saquemos la lotería esta
noche!**

Cross your fingers that we win the lotto tonight!

hacerle al cuento

to exaggerate/make a fuss, lit. to make to the tale

Yo sé que no te dolió; no le hagas al cuento.

I know it didn't hurt you; don't make a fuss.

haber tela de donde cortar

plenty of material, lit. to have fabric out of which to cut

Deberías escribir sobre las andanzas de esa actriz; verás que hay mucha tela de donde cortar.

You should write something about that actress's adventures; there's plenty of material there.

jarabe de pico

lip service, lit. beak's syrup

Ese político nunca hace nada por la gente; es puro jarabe de pico.

That politician never does much for the people; he just gives them lip service.

¡me lleva el diablo!

damn, lit. the devil takes me

¡Me lleva el diablo! Se me olvidó dejarle comida al gato.

Damn! I forgot to leave food out for the cat.

Damn! When something goes wrong and one can't do anything about it, all sources are blamed for this misfortune. The part of the devil in the expression above is sometimes given to other things, as in *¡me lleva la tristeza!* "the sadness takes me," *¡me lleva la que me trajo!* "the one who brought me is taking me back," and the most surprising expression, *¡me lleva el tren!* "the train takes me." *Talk Dirty: Spanish* just hopes you had enough time to buy a ticket first.

mezclar el tocino con la velocidad

to mix two subjects that have nothing to do with each other,
    lit. to mix bacon with speed

No mezcles el tocino con la velocidad.

Don't mix two subjects that have nothing to do with each other.

ni jota

nothing/shit, lit. not even the "j"

Pásame mis gafas porque sin ellas no veo ni jota.

Give me my glasses because without them I don't see shit.

no entender ni la o por lo redondo

to not understand a thing, lit. to not understand even the
    roundness of the letter "o"

**Mi marido dice que, cuando se trata de fútbol, las
    mujeres no entienden ni la o por lo redondo.**

*When it comes to football, my husband insists most women
    don't understand a thing.*

no saber hacer ni la o con un canuto

to not know one's head from one's ass, lit. to not know how to
    make an "o" with a needle

**La despidieron porque no sabía ni hacer ni la o con un
    canuto.**

She was fired because she doesn't know her head from her ass.

ni Dios

nobody, lit. not even God

**Este es el mejor asiento de todo el estadio; ¡de aquí no
    me saca ni Dios!**

*I got the best seat at the stadium; nobody will move me from
    here, not even God!*

Other variations:

ni madres (Mexico)
not a thing, lit. not even mothers

ni pío
not a peep, lit. not even a chirp

ni mú
not a single word, lit. not even "moo"

ni yendo a bailar a Chalma (Mexico)
No f**king way!, lit. not even if you go and dance in Chalma
(a Mexican city where devout people pay respects to the
local saint)
**Este reporte no lo termino mañana ni yendo a bailar a
Chalma.**
There's no f**king way I will finish this report by tomorrow.

No, no, and no way! Here are some expressions you
should learn immediately. Some people take more time
to understand a simple 'no'. Trying to make someone
understand or respect you will give you the opportunity
to increase your colloquial Spanish. If an annoying person doesn't understand the expression *ni yendo a bailar
a Chalma*, then he or she will certainly get one of the
following: *¡ni maíz!* "not even corn," *¡ni loco!* "not even
crazy," and *¡para nada!* "for nothing"—all are alternative
ways to refuse something or show disbelief. *Ni cagando,*
"not even shitting," is vulgar, but the person to whom
you're speaking will certainly get your drift.

no tener vela en el entierro

to have nothing to do with something, lit. to not have a candle
at the burial

**No metan a mi mujer en ese lío; ella no tiene vela en
ese entierro.**

*Don't get my wife involved in that mess; she has nothing to
do with it.*

ni el polvo

without a trace, lit. not even the dust

El ratón se escondió tan rápido que no le vimos ni el polvo.

The mouse hid so fast that seemed disappear without a trace.

sentir pasos en la azotea

to see the writing on the wall, lit. to feel the steps on the roof

**Julián finalmente hizo una cita con su abogado porque
ya sintió pasos en la azotea.**

*Julián finally made an appointment with his lawyer because
now he sees the writing on the wall.*

prendérsele el foco (a alguien)

to have a bright idea, lit. to have one's light bulb go on

**Ayer se me prendió el foco y ya sé qué regalarle a mis
papás para su aniversario.**

*Yesterday I had a bright idea and now I know what to give my
parents as an anniversary gift.*

poner parejo

to reprimand, lit. to put someone even

**Cuando Carla llegó a su casa a las cuatro de la
mañana, su papá la puso pareja.**

*When Carla arrived home at four in the morning, her father
reprimanded her.*

poner (a alguien) como camote

to scold (someone), lit. to put (someone) like a sweet potato

Llegué a la casa diez minutos tarde, y mi mamá me puso como camote.

I got home ten minutes late and my mom scolded me.

poner (a alguien) como campeón

to scold (someone), lit. to put (someone) like a champion

Luisito se hizo pipí en la cama y su mamá lo puso como campeón.

Luisito wet his bed and his mom scolded him.

ponerse las pilas

to get the ball rolling, lit. to put the batteries on

Si quieres ganarte esa beca, tienes que ponerte las pilas.

If you want to get that scholarship, you have to get the ball rolling.

pura paja, f

bullshit, lit. pure straw

Mi profesor de biología siempre habla pura paja.

My biology teacher is always talking bullshit.

sacarse algo de la manga

to pull it out of your ass, lit. to take something out of one's sleeve

Eduardo no tenía un discurso preparado; se lo sacó de la manga.

Eduardo didn't have a planned speech; he pulled it out of his ass.

saludar con sombrero ajeno

to take credit for someone else's work, lit. to greet someone
with someone else's hat

**Yo no confío en mi jefe; siempre está saludando con
sombrero ajeno.**

*I don't trust my boss; he is always taking credit for other's
people work.*

sepa la bola

who knows?, lit. the ball might know

¿Qué quién construyó ese puente? ¡Sepa la bola!

You want to know who built that bridge? Who knows!

chorro, m

lot, lit. spurt

Me duele un chorro

It hurts a lot.

bonche, m

lot, from the English "bunch"

**No me vayas a pisar mi dedo gordo porque lo tengo roto
y me duele un bonche.**

Don't step on my toe; it's broken and hurts a bunch!

montón, m

lot, lit. pile

Lo extraño un montón.

I miss him a lot.

tirar un rollo

to babble on, lit. to throw a roll

Durante la fiesta, Cristina me echó un rollo sobre los hombres casados.

During the party, Christina babbled on about married men.

valer corneta

to go down the drain, lit. to be worth a bugle

Ese matrimonio ya valió corneta.

That marriage went down the drain.

volarse la barda

to go over the top, lit. to go over the fence

¡Mi novio se voló la barda! Me regaló un viaje todo pagado a Europa.

My boyfriend went over the top! He offered me a free trip to Europe.

CHAPTER SIXTEEN

Mamacita:
The Look

Looks are important in Spain, just like everywhere else in the world. Madrid is now a hot European fashion capital, and Spanish designers are rocking the traditional Parisian scene. Cristóbal Balenciaga is a world-renowned twentieth-century master, and anybody who's ever seen *Sex in the City* has heard of the Spanish shoe designer, Manolo Blahnik. Spain has even caused some uproar in the fashion world the banning the use of supermodels under a certain body mass index in Madrid's shows. No worries—anyone too skinny simply needs a day or two to fatten up on *churros* and *paella* to tip the scales in his or her favor.

bien dado, bien dada
vigorous, strong, lit. well given
Lo bueno es que los deportistas están bien dados.
Luckily the athletes are very strong.

buena, bueno
good-looking, lit. good
Los hijos de Maruca están muy buenos.
Maruca's sons are very good-looking.

carita, f

good looking/cute, lit. little face

Scott puede ser muy estúpido, pero es carita.

Scott may be stupid, but he's really cute.

cuero, m

babe, lit. leather

¡George Clooney es un cuero! ¡Es el hombre más guapo del planeta!

George Clooney is babe! He's the most gorgeous man on earth!

cuerpazo, m

nice body, lit. big body

Esa chava es horrible, pero tiene un cuerpazo!

That girl is ugly, but she has such a nice body!

de pipa y guante

very elegant, lit. of pipe and glove

Los invitados llegaron al baile de pipa y guante.

The guests arrived at the ball looking very elegant.

en mangas de camisa

casual dress, lit. in shirt-sleeves

Hacía tanto calor que los banqueros se sacaron el traje para quedar en mangas de camisa.

It was so hot that the bankers ditched their suits and wore casual dress instead.

engendro, m

dog (ugly person), lit. fetus

Enrique es un engendro. ¡No quiero que me vean con él!

Enrique is such a dog. I don't want people to see me with him!

estar como quiere

damn good-looking, lit. to be like one wants

La novia de mi papá está como quiere.

My dad's girlfriend is damn good-looking.

estar en los huesos

to be skin and bones, lit. to be in the bones

Ya dile que coma mejor; está en los huesos.

Tell her to eat more; she's skin and bones.

estar mamado (Mexico)

to be built, lit. to be breastfed

¡El viejo del gimnasio está muy mamado!

The old geezer at the gym is built!

forro, m

hottie, lit. lining

¿Ya vieron a la nueva secretaria? ¡Es un forro!

Have you seen the new secretary? She's a hottie!

mamacita, f

pretty woman, lit. little mother/mommy

¡Mamacita! Llévame contigo!

Pretty woman! Take me with you!

mamita, f

babe, lit. mommy

¡Mamita! Me encanta tu vestido.

Hey babe! I love your dress.

mango, m

peach, lit. mango

Mi prima Melissa está hecha un mango.

My cousin Melissa is a real peach.

mujerón, m

beautiful woman, lit. big woman

La segunda esposa del presidente es un mujerón.

The president's second wife is a beautiful woman.

no cocerse al primer hervor

to be no spring chicken, lit. to not be cooked at the first boil

El chico que conocí en Internet ya no se cuece al primer hervor.

The guy I met online was certainly no spring chicken.

no tener malos bigotes

good-looking, lit. to not have bad moustache

La doctora nueva no tiene malos bigotes.

The new doctor is quite good-looking.

pelo chino, m

curly hair, lit. Chinese hair

Me encantaría tener el pelo chino.

I'd love to have curly hair.

tener los mangos bajitos (Cuba)

to have saggy tits, lit. to have low mangos

Caridad no tiene los mangos bajitos.

Caridad doesn't have saggy tits.

CHAPTER SEVENTEEN

Caes gordo:
Beyond the Look

It's very common, but not very nice, to label people based on the clothes they wear or their looks. *Talk Dirty: Spanish* provides you with all the slang you need to describe their traits. Your travels in friendly Spain and Latin America are sure to make you lots of new *amigos*. From the total loser to the success story, from the social butterfly to the loner, you'll have the vocabulary to stereotype them all.

acojonar (Spain)
to terrify/ intimidate, from *cojones,* "balls"
Esta nueva película de terror te va a acojonar.
This new horror movie is going to terrify you.

boca de verdulero
bad mouth, lit. mouth of a vegetable merchant
**Nora tiene boca de verdulera; se la pasa todo el día
    diciéndole groserías a sus hijos.**
*Nora has a sailor's mouth; she curses at her children all day
    long.*

carrozas (Spain)
old-fashioned, lit. chariots
Mis padres no quieren conectarse a Internet; son un par de carrozas.
My parents don't want to connect to the Web; they are very old-fashioned.

creerse el hoyo del queque (Chile)
to think the world of oneself, lit. to feel one is the hole of the doughnut-shaped cake
Esa actriz se cree el hoyo del queque.
That actress thinks the world of herself.

It's really funny to believe you're the most important person in the world, even if you're a *macho* Latino. In a desert what would you be willing to pay for some water or soda if dying of thirst? *Creerse la última Coca-Cola del desierto,* "to think one is the last Coke in the desert," doesn't need further explanation. *Creerse la última chela del estadio,* "to think one is the last beer in the stadium," is similar, if not even worse for sports fans.

To take the role of death or God and decide who lives and who dies is more than powerful. The phrases c*reerse la muerte* and *creerse Dios,* "to think one is death" and "to think one is God," respectively, refer to people who suffer from a severe superiority complex. *Creerse mucho,* "to think one is very much," and *creerse el muy muy,* "to think one is the very, very," are used for people who act as if they are more important than the rest of humankind.

creerse la divina garza

to think of oneself as the queen bee, lit. to believe one is the
divine heron

Desde que Carla tiene coche, se cree la divina garza.

Since Carla got a car, she thinks she's the queen bee.

caído del catre

stupid, lit. fallen from the cot

**A Roberto no le preguntes nada porque es un caído del
catre.**

Don't ask Roberto anything because he's really stupid.

chapado a la antigua

old-fashioned, lit. old-plated

**Mi tía no es para nada chapada a la antigua. ¡Sale con
un nuevo galán todas las semanas!**

*Old-fashioned can't be used to describe my auntie. She dates
a new young guy every week!*

chupamedias

ass-kisser, lit. stocking sucker

**Alejandro es un chupamedias y por eso la maestra lo
trata bien.**

*Alejandro is an ass-kisser; that's why the teacher treats him
so well.*

caer como bomba

unbearable, lit. to fall like a bomb

**No vayas a invitar a tu primo Juan a la fiesta; me cae
como bomba.**

Don't bring your cousin Juan to the party; he is unbearable.

caer en la punta del hígado

unbearable, lit. to fall on the top of the liver

Las hermanitas Pérez me caen en la punta del hígado.

I can't stand the Pérez sisters.

caer de a madre

unbearable, lit. to fall for the mother

Me cae de a madre que otros me digan lo que tengo que hacer.

I cannot stand when others tell me what to do.

candil de la calle

someone who prefers others outside his or her own kind, lit. street chandelier

El candil de la calle le compró un reloj a su jefe cuando en su casa no hay qué comer.

There's no food at his house, but he bought a watch for his boss.

consentido, consentida

spoiled, lit. consented

Los papás de ese chico siempre le regalan todo; está muy consentido.

That kid's parents give him presents all the time; he is very spoiled.

de hueso colorado

hard-core, lit. of red bone

Mi abuelita es demócrata de hueso colorado.

My granny's a hard-core Democrat.

darse mucho taco

to think the world of oneself, lit. to give oneself a lot of taco

Javier se da mucho taco porque su abuelo fue presidente de la república.

Javier thinks the world of himself because his grandfather was president of the republic.

echarle mucha crema a sus tacos

to spice something up, lit. to put too much cream on one's tacos

Me encanta cómo cuenta mi abuelo las anécdotas, pues le echa mucha crema a sus tacos.

I love the way my Grandpa tells anecdotes; he always spices them up.

entrador, m

courageous/determined, lit. someone who enters

Pídele a Víctor que vaya como tu guardaespaldas; es bien entrador.

Ask Victor to act as your bodyguard; he's really courageous.

estar en la baba

to not pay attention, lit. to be in the drool

Le dije cien veces que viera a la cámara para la foto, pero estaba en la baba.

I told her a hundred times to look into the camera, but she was not paying attention.

estar salado

to have bad luck, lit. to be salty

La mujer de Claudio lo dejó el día que lo despidieron del trabajo; el pobre está salado.

Claudio's wife left him the day he was fired from work; he has such a bad luck.

fresa, f (Mexico)
preppy, lit. strawberry
**Los chavos que van a esa universidad privada son
todos unos fresas.**
The guys that go to that private university are all very preppy.

hacerse el sueco (Spain)
to pretend not to hear, lit. to make oneself the Swedish
**Ya le pregunté mil veces cuándo me va a subir el
sueldo, pero mi jefe se hace el sueco.**
*I asked him a thousand times for a raise, but my boss pretends
not to hear me.*

hacerse el interesante
to make oneself unavailable / to be difficult, lit. to make oneself the interesting one
**Carla no me ha querido contestar el teléfono; se está
haciendo la interesante.**
Carla hasn't picked up her phone; she is being very difficult.

hacerse como que la Virgen le habla
to pretend to not hear or understand something, lit. to make
believe the Virgin is talking to oneself
**¿Dónde estuviste toda la noche? ¡No hagas como que
la Virgen te habla!**
Where were you all night? Don't pretend you don't hear me!

hijo/hija de vecino
just anybody, lit. son/daughter of the neighbor
**Tienes que decirme con quién vas a ir al cine; no quiero
que andes por ahí con cualquier hijo de vecino.**
*You have to tell me who you are going to the movies with; I
don't want you to go out with just anybody.*

infumable

unbearable, lit. unsmokable

La hija de mi jefe es preciosa, pero infumable.

My boss´s daughter is beautiful but unbearable.

mátalas callando

snake, lit. kill them quietly

No confíes en su cara de buena gente; el tipo es mátalas callando.

Don´t be fooled by his nice looks; this guy's a snake.

nacer con la torta bajo el brazo

to be very lucky, lit. to be born with the sandwich under the arm

Ese niño tiene mucha suerte; nació con la torta bajo el brazo.

This kid is very lucky; he was born with a sandwich under his arm.

no dar paso sin huarache

to look out for one's own interests, lit. to not walk without a *huarache* sandal

Los americanos siempre buscan ganar dinero en México; ellos no dan paso sin huarache.

Americans are always looking to make money in Mexico; they're always looking out for their own interests.

no estar ni ahí (Chile)

to pay no attention, lit. to be not even there

La mujer que se sentó a mi lado en el autobús me contó la historia de su vida, pero yo no estaba ni ahí.

The lady sitting next to me on the bus told me her life story, but I paid no attention.

no ser una perita en dulce

to not be the nicest person on earth, lit. to not be a pear in
 syrup

**Se queja del humor de su marido, pero ella no es nin-
 guna perita en dulce.**

*She complains about her husband's bad moods, but she is not
 the nicest person on earth either.*

no tener madre

to have no shame, lit. to have no mother

**Esteban no tiene madre; dice que gana muy poquito
 pero se acaba de comprar coche nuevo.**

*Esteban has no shame; He says he makes very little but just
 bought a new car.*

no tragar a alguien

to dislike someone, lit. to not swallow someone

Pobrecito, nadie lo traga.

Poor guy, nobody likes him.

no poder ver a alguien

to not able to stand someone, lit. to not be able to see
 somebody

Mis suegros no me pueden ni ver.

My in-laws can't stand me.

lit. My in-laws can't see me.

pelusa, f

common people, lit. fluff

**No te juntes con los de este barrio; aquí hay pura
 pelusa.**

*Don't mix with the people of this neighborhood; they're all
 very common.*

pico de cera, m

be quiet/shush, lit. wax beak

Aunque hayas visto quién se robó los dulces . . . tú, ¡pico de cera!

Even though you saw who took the candies . . . be quiet!

ponerse buzo/buza

to be on the look out/pay attention, lit. to put oneself diver

¡Pónte buzo! Cuando digan tu nombre levantas la mano.

Pay attention! When they call out your name, raise your hand.

¡qué bárbaro!

how impressive, lit. how barbaric

¡Qué bárbaro! Terminaste el crucigrama del domingo en apenas veinte minutos.

How impressive! You finished the Sunday crossword puzzle in only twenty minutes.

¡qué concha!

what nerve, lit. what shell

¡Qué concha! La mujer de Carmelo trabajando todo el día y él jugando al dominó.

What nerve! Carmelo's wife works all day while he plays dominos.

¡qué genio!

you're in a bad mood, lit. what a genius

¡Qué genio! Yo sólo te hice una simple pregunta.

Gee, you're in a bad mood! I was just asking you a question.

quemarse

to get a bad reputation, lit. to burn oneself

Te quemaste en la escuela por haber copiado en el examen final.

You got a bad reputation at school after you were caught cheating on the final exam.

sacar de onda

to perplex/disorient someone, lit. to take out of wave

Mi mamá me sacó de onda cuando me dijo que iba a dejar a mi papa.

My mom left me perplexed when she said she was leaving my dad.

sacar canas verdes (a alguien)

to give (someone) grief, lit. to give (someone) green white-hairs

Ese niño es tan travieso que cuando crezca le va a sacar canas verdes a su mamá.

That kid's trouble; he's going to give a lot of grief to his mom.

sacar los trapitos al sol (a alguien)

to expose someone's troubles, lit. to take out the cloth to the sun

Nadia escribió un libro sobre su ex marido, sacándole todos sus trapitos al sol.

Nadia wrote a book about her ex-husband, exposing his problems for all the world to see.

ser un hueso duro de roer

to be difficult, lit. to be a bone difficult to chew

A ver si convences a mi mamá de que me deje dormir esta noche en tu casa, porque es un hueso duro de roer.

Let's see if you can convince my mom to let me sleep over at your house tonight; she is very difficult.

ser un estuche de monerías

to be a jack of all trades, lit. to be a case full of cute things

Mi nana sabe tejer, bordar y cocinar . . . es un estuche de monerías.

My nanny knows how to knit, embroider and cook . . . she's a jack of all trades.

ser muy gente

to be nice/generous, lit. to be very people

La directora es muy gente; siempre ayuda a todos.

The principal is really nice; she is always helping people.

tener la sangre pesada

to be unpleasant, lit. to have heavy blood

No vayas a invitar a Junípero; tiene la sangre pesada.

Don't invite Junípero; he is very unpleasant.

tener la sangre ligera

to be nice/funny, lit. to have light blood

Mi novio a todo mundo le cae bien; ¡tiene la sangre muy ligera!

Everybody seems to like my boyfriend; he's a very nice guy!

tener morro (Spain)

to have nerve, lit. to have snout

¡Qué morro tienes de pedirme dinero cuando todavía me debes!

You gotta lot of nerve! Asking me for a loan when you still owe me money!

tener musgo en el tinaco (Mexico)

somebody who is no longer young, lit. to have moss in the water tank

Mi tía ya no es ninguna jovencita; ya tiene musgo en el tinaco.

My aunt is no longer a young woman; she's no spring chicken.

CHAPTER EIGHTEEN

¡A la chingada!: Send Them Packing

One way to realize you have made it in Mexico is when you can master the concept of *chingada* and can use the term in its multiple forms. *Chingada* itself can mean a prostitute, a promiscuous woman, a place that is very far away; *¡Vete a la Chingada!* means "go f**k yourself." But used with the gerund *–ando,* it usually means to bother (as in *no me estés chingando,* don´t bother me). So, having learned these two forms, you can very well tell someone: *¡no me estés chingando!* or *¡vete a la chingada!* When used with the complement *madre,* "mother," you can then say to someone. *Vete a chingar a tu madre,* which is pretty much the same as telling someone to go f**k themselves!

Other variations:
Eres un hijo de la chingada: You're a son of a bitch.
Ya me tienes hasta la chingada: You have me up to my balls!
Me importa una chingada: I don't give a f**k.
Estás todo dado a la chingada: You're really f**ked up.
Hecho la chingada: Really fast (*Salimos de la fiesta hechos la chingada*).

¡Me lleva la chingada! F**k me!

No estés chingando la marrana: Stop f**king around.

Me di un chingadazo con la puerta: I bumped myself against the door.

¡Esas son chingaderas!: That´s f**king bullshit!

Me duele un chingo: It f**king hurts.

No me chingues: Don't f**k around with me.

Son todos unos chinga-quedito: You're all little f**k-ups.

However, you can also use the word to show immense respect to people:

Eres un chingón: You kick ass!

Mi moto está bien chingona: My motorcycle is so f**king cool.

Yo soy el más chingón del mundo: I am the king of the world.

Esa foto es una chingonería: That photo is f**king amazing!

¡al diablo!
to hell!, lit. to the devil

¡Al diablo con mi familia! Me voy a vivir con Juan.

To hell with my family! I'm moving in with Juan.

andar a cagar
to go to hell, lit. to go to shit

¡Anda a cagar! No te creo nada de lo que me dices.

Get out of here! I don't believe a word of what you are saying.

cantarle las cuarenta (a alguien) (Spain)
to tell somebody off, lit. to sing the forty to someone

No me ha querido dar la cara, pero en cuanto lo vea le voy a cantar las cuarenta.

She hasn't dared to face me, but as soon as I see her I will vent.

cerrar el pico

to shut up, lit. to close the beak

Cierra el pico y déjame ver la película.

Shut up and let me watch the movie.

dar en la madre

to beat someone/ruin something, lit. to give in the mother

¡Mira cómo dejaste mi coche! Le diste en toda la madre.

Look what you´ve done to my car! You have ruined it.

dar lata

to bother someone, lit. to give can

Ya no me estés dando lata; no te voy a comprar ese juguete.

Stop bothering me; I will not buy you that toy.

dejar la cagada

to leave a mess, lit. to leave the shit

El último huracán dejó la cagada en el Caribe.

The last hurricane left a mess in the Caribbean.

dejar la crema

to leave a mess/f**k up something, lit. to leave the cream

El presidente renunció – por fin – después de dejar la crema en el país.

The president finally quit, after he f**ked up everything in the country.

hasta el copete/la coronilla

up to here, lit. up to the tuft/crown

Deja de cantar esa canción; ya me tienes hasta el copete.

Stop singing that song; I've had it up to here with you.

hinchar

to bother, lit. to swell up

¡Ya te dije que no me estés hinchando!

I told you to stop bothering me!

lit. I told you to stop swelling me up!

hinchar las pelotas

to bother someone, lit. to fill up someone's balls

Ve a molestar a otra parte; no me hinches las pelotas.

Go pester someone else; don't bother me.

oler a demonios

to stink, lit. to smell of demons

Llévense a bañar a este niño; ¡huele a demonios!

Take this kid to the shower; He stinks!

oler a rayos

to stink!, lit. to smell of lightning

¿No te bañaste hoy? ¡Hueles a rayos!

Didn´t you take a shower today? You stink!

mandarle a freír espárragos (a alguien)

to leave someone, lit. to send someone to fry asparagus

Mi novio me mandó a freir espárragos.

My boyfriend dumped me.

mandar le con su música a otra parte (a alguien)

to send somebody away, lit. to send someone with his/her
    music elsewhere

**La vecina vino a insistir que fuéramos a la iglesia, pero
    la mandamos con su música a otra parte.**

*The neighbor came over to insist we go to church, but we sent
    her packing.*

Other variations include:

mandarle a la goma (a alguien)
to send (someone) packing, lit. to send (someone) to the rubber

mandarle a volar (alguien)
to send (someone) packing, lit. to send (someone) flying

mandarle por un tubo (alguien)
to send (someone) packing, lit. to send through a tube

Catholicism is the base for Hispanic culture, and as a result a person banned from society is naturally sent to the devil. To send people to hell just use *¡vete al diablo!*, "go to the devil!"; *¡vete al demonio!*, "go to the demon!"; *vete al cuerno!*, "go to the horn!"; or *¡vete a la tostada!*, "go to the toast!" With the crowd already in hell, maybe the one you want to get rid of won't find a space there. There's an indirect way to send them to hell, making them commit sins . . . *¡Vete a la chingada!*, is a classic, while *¡vete a la perica!*, literally "go to the female parrot!" is more obscure and dubious.

Laziness is sometimes a cause of anger. A lazybones who's always on your back is quite annoying. Work is then the best solution: you can use *¡vete a la goma!*, literally "go to the rubber," or *¡vete a hacer puñetas!*, "go and make lace cuffs." Sometimes it's not the personality that annoys. People are sent away because they stink and the others can't handle it anymore; *¡vete a bañar!*, literally, "go take a shower!" is certainly one of the cleanest ways to send someone packing.

¡no mames/manches!

get outta here, lit. do not suck/stain

¡No mames! No puedo creer que pagaste $2,000 por ese coche.

Get outta here! Don't tell me you paid $2,000 for that car.

no romper un plato

to be harmless, lit. to not break break a plate

Mírale la carita a esa niña; parece que no rompe un plato.

Look at that cute little girl; she looks harmless but I'm sure she's trouble.

pegarle una hostia (a alguien)

to beat/smack (somebody), to give (someone) a host

Cuando Juanito le dijo a su mamá que era una cualquiera, ésta le pegó una hostia.

When Juanito told his mom she was a hooker, she smacked him.

pelearse con Sansón a las patadas

to fight with someone stronger than us, lit. to fight Samson by kicking him

Los punks se quisieron pelear con los guaruras, pero eso era como ponerse con Sansón a las patadas.

The punks wanted to fight with the security guards, but there's no way they would've won.

pintar le un violin (a alguien)

to give (someone) the finger, lit. to paint a violin

Le dijimos que era muy feo y nos pintó un violín.

We told him he was ugly and he gave us the finger.

valer gorro

to give a damn, lit. to be worth a hat

Dicen que Miranda anda hablando mal de mí, pero me vale gorro.

They say Miranda is saying bad things about me but I don't give a damn.

valer queso

to be worthless, lit. to be worth cheese

Mi coche valió queso; ya no arranca más.

My car was worthless; it wouldn't start anymore.

valer un pepino

to not care, lit. to give the value of a cucumber

Me vale un pepino si no me quieres.

I don't give a damn if you don't love me.

Annoying people usually find everthing they say extremely interesting and don't seem to understand that you could care less. There's no secret formula to stop them, but Spanish idioms provide a way to make the person understand your lack of interest. If the dude doesn't understand *me vale gorro / me vale pepino* then just change the object with another of these useless or worthless items: *bolillo* (bread), *cacahuate* (peanut), *callampa* (mushroom), *corneta* (bugle), *comino* (cumin), *rábano* (radish), *camote* (sweet potato), *chorizo* (sausage), *sombrilla* (umbrella), *pimiento* (pepper), *pito* (dick). If this doesn't do the trick, your pest is either deaf or just doesn't give a damn.

mandarle a ver si ya puso la marrana (a alguien)
to send (someone) to hell, lit. to send (someone) to go see if
the pig has given birth
**Mi hermano me vino a molestar pero le dije que fuera a
ver si ya puso la marrana.**
My brother came to bother me, but I told him to go to hell.

CHAPTER NINETEEN

Por la calle de la amargura:
To Love and Be Loved

If there's one stereotype that surrounds Latino men, it's their red-hot streak. When this comes to love or sex, this means a reputation as some of the world's greatest lovers. Passionate and sensual, Latinos are "manly" men . . . and many women's ideal lovers. Oozing testosterone, who could resist these charming and protective men? Certainly not *gringas* used to men afraid of public displays of affection and leery of romance. Most important, Latinos break the final barrier of American men—they dance . . . and actually enjoy it.

This image didn't appear from nowhere—it has been nurtured and promoted throughout the last few decades years by several important Spanish and Latino stars, including Julio Iglesias, Antonio Banderas, and Ricky Martin. With their sultry looks and playboy personas, these guys have done more to secure the sexy status of Hispanics worldwide than Bill Gates has done for computer geeks.

andar

to go out with someone, lit. to go

Yo creo que mi prima anda con Julio.

I think my cousin is going out with Julio.

batear por la izquierda

to play for the other team/to be gay, lit. to bat with the
    left arm

**Con esos pantalones ajustados verdes parece que
    bateas por la izquierda.**

*With those tight green pants you look like you play for the
    other team.*

cachetear las banquetas

to be crazy about someone, lit. to smack one's cheeks against
    the curb

**¡Mi profesor de literatura me tiene cacheteando las
    banquetas!**

I am crazy about my literature professor!

casa chica

love nest, lit. small house

**Todo el mundo sabe que el director de la compañía le
    puso casa chica a la secretaria.**

Everybody knows the CEO set up a love nest for his secretary.

cornudo, cornuda

cheated on person, lit. horned one

**Todo el mundo sabe que José es un cornudo, ¡y él está
    furioso!**

*Everybody knows José's is being cheated on, and he's pissed
    about it!*

cortar

to break up, lit. to cut

Mi novia está tan enojada que creo que me va a cortar.

My girlfriend is so mad that I think she'll break up with me.

dar bola

to pay attention to someone, lit. to give someone a ball

¡Ese chico no me da bola!

That guy doesn't pay attention to me!

dar entrada

to welcome someone's advances, lit. to give entry

Sé que tu hermana tiene novio, pero igual a mí me dio entrada.

I know your sister has a boyfriend, but still, she welcomed my advances.

darle la hora (a alguien) (Chile)

to give someone the time of day, lit. to give out the time

Me encanta la hija del vecino, pero no me da ni la hora.

I like the neighbor's daughter a lot, but she doesn't give me the time of day.

darle calabazas (a alguien)

to leave someone, lit. to give someone squash

La novia de Charlie le dio calabazas y se casó con otro.

Charlie's girlfriend left him and married another man.

dejarle plantado (a alguien)

to stand someone up, lit. to plant somebody

Estuve esperándola tres horas en el café pero me dejó plantado.

I waited for her three hours at the café but she stood me up.

dejarse querer

to let oneself be loved

Me fascina Carlito, pero no se deja querer.

I really like Carlito, but he doesn't let himself be loved.

de lengüita

French kiss, lit. of little tongue

Mi novio y yo nos besamos de lengüita.

My boyfriend and I French kiss each other using the tongue.

echar novio/novia

to go out with one's boyfriend/girlfriend, lit. to throw a
     boyfriend/girlfriend

**Dolores se salió desde temprano; seguro está echando
     novio.**

*Dolores left early this morning; I'm sure she's with her
     boyfriend.*

echarle los perros (a alguien) (Mexico)

to flirt with someone, lit. to throw the dogs (at someone)

**Desde que llegamos al baile, este chavo me está
     echando los perros.**

Since we arrived at the ball, the guy has been flirting with me.

estar cachondo/caliente

to be horny, lit. to be horny/hot

El tipo que trabaja en la sex shop está cachondo.

The guy that works at the sex shop is really horny.

estar tragado (Colombia)

to be crazy about someone, lit. to be swallowed

Roberto está tragado por su vecina.

Roberto is crazy about his neighbor.

flechazo, m

love at first sight, lit. arrow shot

Fue un verdadero flechazo; ese mismo día nos comprometimos.

It was love at first sight; that same day we got engaged.

hacer agua la canoa

to play for the other team/to be gay, lit. to make water the canoe

Chicas, olvídense de coquetear con Mike; a él le hace agua la canoa.

Don't bother flirting with Mike, girls—he plays for the other team.

hacer mosca

to be the third wheel, lit. to make fly

Mejor los dejé solos en el cine, porque yo nada más estaba haciendo mosca.

I left them alone at the movies because I was just the third wheel.

jugar a los dos bandos (Cuba)

to be bisexual, lit. to play on both sides

Creo que tu primo juega a los dos bandos.

I think your cousin is bisexual.

lagartona, f

cougar, craddle-robber, lit. big female lizard

Esa señora siempre sale con jovencitos; es una lagartona.

That lady is always dating younger men; she's a cougar.

ligar

to flirt, lit. to tie up

Anoche en la fiesta me ligué a tres chavos.

At last night's party I flirted with three guys.

llegarle (a alguien)

to declare one's love to (someone), lit. to arrive (at someone)

Ya me decidí. Hoy le voy a llegar a la chica de quinto año.

I've decided that today I will declare my love to the girl in fifth grade.

media naranja, f

soulmate, other half, lit. half an orange

A ver si durante mis vacaciones en España encuentro a mi media naranja.

Let's see if during my vacation in Spain I can meet my soulmate.

mover el tapete

to stir someone's feelings, lit. to move the rug

Mi cuñado me mueve el tapete, pero por el bien de mi hermana, mejor no digo nada.

I'm really attracted to my brother-in-law, but for my sister's sake I keep it to myself.

movida, f

lover, lit. move

Sí voy a ir a tu fiesta, pero no con mi esposa; voy a llevar a mi movida.

Yes, I'll come to your party, but I will not bring my wife. I'm coming with my mistress instead.

no fumarse (a alguien)

to ignore (someone), lit. to not smoke (somebody)

Siempre me porto muy bien en la escuela para complacer a mi papá, pero él ni me fuma.

I do well in school to please my dad, but he ignores me.

no pelarse (a alguien)

to not pay attention (to somebody), lit. to not peel (somebody)

Siempre le compro cosas a Carlos, pero él ni me pela.

I'm always buying things for Carlos, but he doesn't pay attention.

no tentarse el corazón

heartlessly/without compassion, lit. to not touch one's heart

La maestra nos reprobó a todos sin tocarse el corazón.

The teacher failed us all heartlessly.

lit. The teacher failed us all without touching her heart.

patas negras, patas de lana (Chile)

lover, other one, lit. black feet, woolen feet

¡No me lo vas a creer! La vecina dejó a su marido por el patas de lana.

You won't believe this! The neighbor left her husband for her lover.

petacona, f (Mexico)

woman with junk in the trunk, lit. big suitcase

Me encanta el cuerpo de mi novia porque está muy petacona.

I love my girlfriend's body because she's got junk in the trunk.

quedada

single woman/old maid, lit. leftover

Carlota es una quedada; ya tiene cuarenta años y no tiene ni novio.

Carlota is an old maid; she's already forty and she doesn't even have a boyfriend.

quedarse a vestir santos

to be an old maid/confirmed bachelor, lit. to dress up the saints

¡Pobre mujer! Si no se casa pronto, se va a quedar a vestir santos.

Poor woman! She'll die an old maid if she doesn't marry soon.

querida, f

mistress, lit. dear one

El doctor llegó al teatro con su querida.

The doctor arrived at the theatre with his mistress.

resbalosa

loose, lit. slippery

Me cae muy mal esa muchacha; es una resbalosa.

I don't like that girl; she's loose.

sancho

lover, lit. Sancho, as in Don Quijote's sidekick

Creo que el marido de mi profesora no va a venir a la fiesta; pues ella está aquí con Sancho.

I think my professor's husband is not coming to the party; tonight she's here with her lover.

segundo frente

lover, mistress, lit. second front

Seguro Manuel no viene porque hoy le toca visitar a su segundo frente.

Manuel surely will not show up because today he visits his mistress.

taco de ojo, m

eye candy, lit. eye taco

Los chicos de la clase de gimnasia no son muy inteligentes, pero son buenos para un taco de ojo.

The guys at gym class are not too smart, but they're good eye candy.

traerle por la calle de la amargura (a alguien)

to make somebody suffer for love, lit. to have (somebody) along the street of bitterness

Mariana trae a su novio por la calle de la amargura.

Mariana really makes her boyfriend suffer.

tener corazón de alcachofa

to be good-hearted, lit. to have an artichoke heart

Verónica nunca va a decir nada malo de sus suegros; tiene corazón de alcachofa.

Verónica will never say anything bad about her in-laws; she is very good-hearted.

tener corazón de condominio

to have lots of lovers, lit. to have a condominium heart

Claudia anda con muchos chicos a la vez; tiene corazón de condominio.

Claudia is with several guys at the same time.

tortolitos, pl

lovebirds, lit. turtledoves

Mira los tortolitos; siempre se están besando en público.

Look at the lovebirds; they are always kissing in public.

andar tras los huesos (de alguien)

to be after somebody, lit. after (someone's) bones

Hace como cinco años que Carlos anda tras los huesos de Catalina.

It's been over five years that Carlos has been after Catalina.

viejo verde

cradle-robber, lit. green old man

Ray ya tiene sesenta años y le gustan las jovencitas; es un viejo verde.

Ray's sixty years old but likes young women; he's a cradle-robber.

CHAPTER TWENTY

Echando un polvo:

Dirty, Dirtier, and Dirtiest Spanish

As a connoisseur, you have certainly kept this section for dessert, the *churros* of *Talk Dirty: Spanish*. If you have chosen to start the book with this section, you're the kind that of person that eats dessert first. In any case welcome to the dark side, the dirtiest part of the Spanish language. Words and expresiones to see you through the pleasures of sex and masturbation will be found below. Rather than provide detailed information, *Talk Dirty: Spanish* has a quantity over quality approach—this *capítulo* is longer than the rest for a reason!

acabar
to come, lit. to finish
¡Estaba a punto de acabar, cuando el maldito se salió!
XXX: To Dirty to Translate

acostarse
to have sex, lit. to lay down
Yo pienso que Carlos y su novia ya se acostaron.
I think Carlos and his girlfriend have already had sex.

aflojar

to go to bed, lit. to come loose

Esa chava es muy fácil; luego afloja con los chavos.

That girl is very easy; she goes to bed with guys right away.

lit. That girl is very easy; she loosens up with guys quickly.

bicho (Puerto Rico)

dick, lit. small insect

**Sin afán de ofender, tu bicho huele como si no te lo
hubieses lavado en mucho tiempo.**

XXX: To Dirty to Translate

bizcocho, m

pussy, lit. biscuit

**Steve le rogó a Carmelita para que le mostrara el
bizcocho.**

XXX: To Dirty to Translate

cabecear

to give head, from *cabeza,* "head"

**Pese a tener tan lindos labios, a Silvia no le gusta
cabecear.**

XXX: To Dirty to Translate

cachapera, f (Venezuela)

lesbian, from *cachapa,* "corn patty"

Este bar es el predilecto de las cachaperas.

This bar is mostly frequented by lesbians.

calientapollas

cock-tease, lit. cock-heater

Las muchachas de mi barrio son todas unas calientapollas.

The girls from my neighborhood are all cock-teases.

chichis, mpl (Mexico)

breasts, from the Náhuatl *chichi*, "to suck"

Bárbara se veía muy bonita, pero yo pienso que se puso chichis falsas.

Bárbara looked very pretty, but I think her breasts are fake.

chucha, f (Chile)

cunt, lit. female dog or possum

Cuando Juana se puso ese vestido volado, se le veía toda la chucha.

XXX: To Dirty to Translate

chuparle la polla (a alguien)

to suck someone's dick, lit to suck (someone's) hen

Sienna le chupó la polla a su novio en la segunda cita.

XXX: To Dirty to Translate

coger (Mexico)

to f**k, lit. to grab

Esmeralda se coge a cualquier tipo rico que se le atraviese por ahí.

*Esmeralda f**ks any rich guy she can get her legs around.*

cojones, plm (Spain)

balls

No tiene cojones para decírselo.

He doesn't have the balls to say that.

When it comes to Mexico forget about *cojones,* here it's all about *huevos* "eggs," also spelled *güevos*, which is how balls are known. And balls, or eggs, are part of many expressions. Some examples: *¡A huevo!,* "the hell it's right!" literally "to egg"; *costar un huevo y la mitad del otro,* "to cost a fortune" literally "to cost one ball and the half of the other ball (egg)"; *me importa un huevo,* "I don't give a damn," literally "I care a ball (an egg)"; and *¡Huevos!,* "F**k you!," literally "balls!"

joder
to f**k
Mi novia y yo jodemos mucho.
My girlfriend and I f**k a lot.

correrse
to come, lit. to run oneself
Dicen que la mujer lo dejó porque se corría muy rápido.
XXX: To Dirty to Translate

culo, m
ass
Jennifer Lopez tiene el culo más jugoso de todo Nueva York.
Jennifer Lopez has the hottest ass in all of New York.

IMMIGRATION OFFICER
★ (3298) ★
24 MAY 2003

Coño, cunt, deserves its own phrase book as it is widely used throughout the Spanish-language word to spice up all sorts of situations and to explain and support phrases. Although it is more commonly used to explain the female genitals, *coño* is used in several situations, including some of the following:

> *¿Dónde coño dejé las llaves?* Where the hell did I leave my keys?
>
> *¿Qué coño te pasa?* What the hell is wrong with you?
>
> *¡Coño, tengo hambre!* Damn, I am hungry!
>
> *¿Vienes de una vez, coño?* For God's sake, are you coming or not?
>
> *¡Este tío es un verdadero coñazo!* This guy is a real pain in the ass!
>
> *¿Qué coños quieres?* What the f**k do you want?
>
> *Ese tío está encoñado con su prima.* The guy is obsessed with his cousin.

darlas
to give it up, lit. to give them out
Después de tres meses de salir con Gregorio, María finalmente se las dio.
After three months of dating Gregorio, María finally gave it up.

doña Manuela, f
hand job, lit. Mrs. Manuela (from the word *mano,* "hand")
Ya sabes lo que dicen por ahí; a todos los chavos les gusta hacerse una Manuela.
You know what they say: all guys love hand jobs.

echar un polvo (Spain)

to f**k, lit. to throw a dust

¡Si no echo un polvo por lo menos tres veces por semana, me vuelvo loco!

If I don't f**k at least three times a week I get crazy!

echarse un palo, m

to f**k, lit. to throw a stick

Se echaron un palo en el coche en la primera cita.

They had sex in the car on their first date.

follar (Spain)

to f**k; to fold

Nunca folles sin condón.

Never f**k without a condom!

foquin (Puerto Rico)

to f**k, from the English *f**k*

Yo quiero hacer foquin con mi novia, pero quiere llegar virgen al matrimonio.

I would like to f**k my girlfriend, but she wants save herself for marriage.

hacerse una puñeta (Spain)

to jerk off, lit. to make oneself a *puñeta*, meaning "jerk" or "bore"

A Javier lo cacharon haciéndose una puñeta durante su clase de español.

Javier was caught jerking off during Spanish class.

hacerse una chaqueta

to jerk off, lit. to make oneself a jacket

**Lo castigaron una semana, porque su mamá lo agarró
haciéndose una chaqueta.**
*He was grounded for a week after his mother caught him jerk-
ing off.*

hacerse una paja
to masturbate, lit. to make a straw
Tan chiquito y ya haciéndose pajas . . .
So young, and already masturbating . . .

impermeable, m
condom, lit. raincoat
**El doctor que curó a Nicolas de la sífilis, le advirtió que
para la próxima, se ponga impermeable.**
*The doctor who cured Nicolas's syphilis told him to use a
condom next time.*

lolas, plf (Argentina)
tits, lit. breasts
**A Lucía le encanta mostrar las lolas a los chicos del
barrio.**
Lucía loves to show her tits to the kids in the neighborhood.

melones, plm
breasts, lit. melons
**Julieta no sólo canta bien sino que tiene unos tremen-
dos melones.**
Not only Julieta is a great singer, she has fantastic breasts.

mojar el bizcocho (Spain)
to dip one's wick, lit. to wet the cookie
¡Pobre! Lleva un mes sin mojar el bizcocho.
Poor guy, he's gone a month without dipping his wick.

If the Catholic Church is against the use of condoms except in specific and rare occasions, Hispanics have found a way to both follow the holy recommendations and offer themselves protection against diseases, unwanted pregnancies, and risk of death. The trick is to not use a "condom," but rather one of its euphemisms. Come rain or come shine, *un impermeable,* literally "a raincoat," should always be carried with you. In bed, don't forget your clean *forro,* "linen" (Spain). In the same conditions, *un sombrero de Panamá* (Mexico), "Panamanian sombrero," shouldn't be forgotten either. Even in a peaceful country, *un casco,* "helmet," should always be kept close by. But if war is declared, and you're out then just take out of your pocket the effigy of your *ángel custodio* or *ángel de la guarda,* "guardian angel," and pray.

mojar el carbón
to have sex, lit. to wet the charcoal
Nada más ven una mujer en bikini y ya quieren mojar el carbón.
As soon as the guys see a girl in bikini, they want to have sex with her.

pájaro, pajarito, m
penis, lit. bird
A Manuel se le abrió el cierre de la bragueta y se le vio todo el pájaro ¡Guácala!
The zipper of Manuel's pants opened up and you could see his penis. Gross!

panocha (Mexico)

pussy, lit. sweet bread or brown sugar candy

Fernanda me pidió que le rasurara la panocha.

XXX: To Dirty to Translate

papaya, f

pussy, lit. papaya

Bonita le rasuró la papaya a su prima cuando ésta se emborrachó.

XXX: To Dirty to Translate

petaca, f (Mexico)

butt-cheek, lit. suitcase

Me encantan esos pantalones; se me ven muy grandes las petacas.

I love these pants; my butt-cheeks look big in them.

pepita, f

clit, lit. seed/nugget

A Alicia le gusta cuando su novio acaricia su pepita.

XXX: To Dirty to Translate

pico (Chile)

dick, lit. peak

Jaime siempre está comparando el tamaño de su pico con el de su hermano.

Jaime is always comparing the size of his dick with his brother's.

pillar en el ajo (Spain)

to catch somebody in the act, lit. to catch in the garlic

Mi marido nos pilló en el ajo.

My husband caught us in the act.

pito (Mexico)
cock, lit. whistle
**El jefe de mi hermana es un asqueroso; siempre se está
rascando el pito.**
My sister's boss is disgusting; he is always scratching his cock.

plátano, m
dick, lit. banana
**El bailarín del club se sacó el plátano en plena
actuación.**
*The club dancer took out his dick in the middle of the
performance.*

polla (Spain)
cock, lit. female chicken
¡El tío tiene una polla impresionante!
That guy has an amazing dick!

polvo, m
f**k, lit. powder
Vamos a echar un polvo antes de ir al cine.
Let's have sex before going to the movies.

pompas, fpl
butt, lit. pumps
**Me encantan estos pantalones porque se me ven muy
bien las pompas.**
I love these pants because they make my ass look great!

ponerle el gorro a alguien (Chile)
to be unfaithful, lit. to put on the cap/hat
**Qué bueno que Ricardo dejó a su novia; hacía meses
que ella le ponía el gorro.**

It's good that Ricardo finally left his girlfriend; she had been cheating on him for months.

In Spanish, there is certainly no lack of words to describe the male appendage. In a culture that tends make sex taboo, people have invented an amazing amount of expressions for their intimate parts. Images of any kind present themselves as a way to avoid the harshness of using the clinical terms. That's when it becomes interesting. . . . Entomologists will ask you to handle with extreme care their very rare and precious *bicho,* "small insect." Some Mexican musician will try to teach you how to play *el pito,* "the whistle." Certainly inspired by the surrounding *Cordilleras de los Andes,* Chileans, in a moment of great humility, will suggest you to climb *el pico,* "the peak." And be warned that being offered to see *el pájaro,* "the bird," *el pajarito,* or the "little bird" doesn't involve a visit to the ornithological garden, or the "horny-tological" garden.

ponerle los cuernos (a alguien)
to cheat on someone, lit. to put the horns
Cada vez que mi mejor amigo sale de viaje, le pone los cuernos a su esposa.
My best friend cheats on his wife every time he takes a business trip.

rapidín, m
quickie, lit. small quick
Nos echamos un rapidín a la hora del almuerzo.
We had a quickie at lunch time.

romper el tambor
to deflower, lit. to break the drum
Alina tenía diecisiete años cuando se dejó romper el tambor por su novio.
Alina was seventeen when she allowed her boyfriend to deflower her.

sacarle la vuelta (a alguien)
to cheat on someone, lit. to take out the turn
Lydia tiene cara de que no rompe un plato, pero esa mujer le saca la vuelta al marido.
Lydia looks really innocent, but that woman cheats on her husband.
lit. Lydia has the face of he who doesn't break a plate, but she takes the turn out of her husband.

soplar
to bang/f**k, lit. to blow
David es el tipo de chavo que se soplaría a su hermana sin pedirle permiso a su mamá.
David is the kind of guy who'd bang his sister without asking his mom for permission.

tirar
to f**k, lit. to throw
Esa pinche vieja se tiró a mi novio.
XXX: To Dirty to Translate

BIBLIOGRAPHY

da Silva, Guido Goméz. *Diccionario breve de mexicanismos.* Mexico City, Mexico: Fondo de Cultura Económica, 2001.

Gálvez, Jose, Hastings, Andrew, Editors. *Spanish Phrasebook.* Paris, France: Larousse, 2006.

Jiménez, Armando. *Tumbaburros de la Picardía Mexicana.* Mexico City, Mexico: Editorial Diana, 1977.

Mahler, Michael. *Dictionary of Spanish Slang.* Hauppage, New York: Barron's Educational Series, Inc., 2000.

http://www.about.com

http://www.answers.com

http://www.bbc.co.uk/languages/spanish/cool/

http://www.jergasdehablahispana.org

http://www.languagerealm.com/spanish/spanishslang

http://www.mrgabe.com/dictionary/Spanish/

http://www.notam02.no/~hcholm/altlang/

http://www.wikipedia.com

http://www.wordreference.com

ABOUT THE AUTHORS

Alexis Munier (Lausanne, Switzerland) relocated to Europe in her mid-twenties and began teaching English at world-renown language schools in Russia, Slovenia, and Italy. There, she learned the difficulties of infusing classic language study with the true native form. Now a writer and opera singer, Ms. Munier still finds time to perfect her French slang and swoon from her Swiss husband's flattery now and again. Ms. Munier spends her free time in sunny Andalusia, Spain, where she is learning to *salsa* like a native and make authentic *paella*.

Laura Martínez (New York, New York) has lived and worked as a journalist in Mexico City, Santiago de Chile, and Buenos Aires. She found her true second home in New York City, where she has survived a terrorist attack, massive blackout, neighborhood pipe explosion and the transformation of Times Square into Disney World. Ms. Martínez lives *la vida loca* in Harlem with her *franchute* boyfriend.